TAN AI-GIRL

EXPLORING CHILDREN'S PERCEPTIONS OF LEARNING

TEACHING AND LEARNING SERIES

Marshall Cavendish
Academic

© 2004 Marshall Cavendish International
(Singapore) Private Limited

Published 2004 by Marshall Cavendish Academic
An imprint of Marshall Cavendish International
(Singapore) Private Limited
A member of Times Publishing Limited

Times Centre, 1 New Industrial Road,
Singapore 536196
Tel:(65) 6213 9288
Fax: (65) 6284 9772
E-mail: mca@sg.marshallcavendish.com
Website:
http://www.marshallcavendish.com/academic

ISBN: 981-210-413-5

A CIP catalogue record for this book is available from
the National Library Board (Singapore).

Printed by Times Graphics Pte Ltd, Singapore
on non-acidic paper

London • New York • Beijing • Shanghai
• Bangkok • Kuala Lumpur • Singapore

Marshall Cavendish Academic

TEACHING AND LEARNING SERIES
Series Editor: Jason Tan

This series focuses on a variety of issues related to teaching and learning. It seeks to promote awareness of indigenous research conducted on these two areas amid the current trend of education reform initiatives in the Asia-Pacific region.

Other Titles in the Series

- Creativity for Teachers *by Tan Ai-girl* and *Law Lai-chong*
- Family Matters *by Lana Khong Yiu-lan*
- Personal Agency Beliefs in Self-regulation: The Exercise of Personal Responsibility, Choice, and Control in Development *by Chong Wan-har*
- Interactive Learning for School Leaders *by David Ng Foo-seong*
- Academic Self-concept in a Streamed Setting *by Liu Woon Chia* and *John Wang Chee-keng*
- Educating the Malaysian Scientist: A Partnership of Science, Nature, and Culture *by Tan Sok-khim*
- Pedagogical Content Knowledge (PCK): All Teachers Need to Know This! *by Ho Boon-tiong*
- Teachers in the 21st Century *by Tan Ai-girl* and *Law Lai-chong*
- The Learning School *by Ng Pak-tee*

CONTEMPORARY ISSUES IN EDUCATION SERIES
Series Editors: Jason Tan and Mok Ka-ho

This series focuses on contemporary issues in education within the Asia-Pacific region. It draws upon the growing body of research being conducted on a variety of issues.

Other Titles in the Series

- Reflective Practice in Malaysian Teacher Education: Assumptions, Practices, and Challenges *by Lee Wai-heng* and *Tan Sok-khim*
- Creating Education Dreams *by Trivina Kang Lu-ming*
- Transition from School to Work: Individual Life Courses within Social Structures *by Chew Siew-ghee*
- Educational Practice in Leadership Mentoring: The Singapore Experience *by Lim Lee Hean*
- Globalization and Higher Education in East Asia *edited by Mok Ka-ho* and *Richard James*
- Class Size Reduction in East Asia *edited by Ip Kin-yuen* and *Lai Kwok-chan*

About the Series Editors

JASON TAN is Associate Professor, Policy & Management Studies Group, National Institute of Education, Nanyang Technological University, Singapore.

MOK KA-HO is Associate Professor and Associate Dean (Education), Faculty of Humanities and Social Sciences, City University of Hong Kong.

Contents

This book is dedicated to our children
Ming-han, Jun-yee, Lu-hern, Jye-chyi and Chiat-hsien
who have engaged us actively in listening to their voices

Acknowledgements

Words of thanks are due to the following persons. Without their encouragement and trust in educational and academic research, this book project would not have been completed so smoothly. All flaws found in this book are due to my shortcomings in presenting a thorough overview of what children's views are. I take the sole responsibility.

- Children and teachers in the primary and secondary schools for their participation.
- Cheng Mun-mun for her willingness to take part in an interview.
- Yong Huai-sin and Lee Ming-han for data collection and data entry.
- Tan Oon-seng for his foreword and for entrusting me to chair the departmental PhD and postgraduate examinations.
- Allan Luke for inviting me to attend project meetings, retreat and talks of the Centre for Research in Pedagogy and Practice.
- Jason Tan Eng-thye for series editor's comments.
- Lim Kam-ming for peer review.
- Asia Pacific Education Review for permitting us to reprint our paper.
- Marshall Cavendish Academic Publishing team, especially Anthony Thomas, Roy See and Karin Seet for their editorial expertise.
- My family for their support and love.

About the Author

Tan Ai-girl is an associate professor of the National Institute of Education (Psychological Studies), Nanyang Technological University, Singapore. Her main research interests include creativity, problem solving, culture and psychology, and multicultural education.

About the Co-authors

Dianaros A. Majid is a primary school teacher and a Ph.D. candidate of the National Institute of Education (Psychological Studies).

Hong Ee-li was a faculty of the National Institute of Education (Psychological Studies).

Lim Ai-hua is a student teacher of the Bachelor degree program at the National Institute of Education.

Raslinda Rasidir is a primary school teacher. She completed her Master degree in Education at the National Institute of Education.

Tan Chee-yuen completed his Master degree in Law at the University of Melbourne, Australia.

Yee Woei-chee, Flora is a choir instructor for secondary school students. She completed her Master of Arts in Applied Psychology at the National Institute of Education.

Foreword

What should we do with children that would be in the best interest of children? We may articulate desired competencies and describe a vision of what children need to be taught. Or we may argue that instructions that are externally imposed and structured do not really address the individual child's curiosity and problems. One thing that is clear, whether we address issues pertaining to children's curricula or challenges of meeting their unique needs—we should not forget to hear the concerns from children themselves.

About a year ago I visited the Archives Jean Piaget at the University of Geneva and had a wonderful time conversing with Professor Jacques Vonèche (who co-authored *The Essential Piaget* with Professor Howard Gruber). As we spoke about the works of Piaget and his life we came to realise that Piaget was able to provide the world with wealth of knowledge about the child's mind, thoughts and worldviews because of his unceasing interactions with children. As educators, psychologists and education researchers we need to continue this legacy of understanding children through intense interactions with them using proven and innovative research paradigms. *Exploring Children's Perceptions of Learning* is thus a much needed and timely publication. The book captures key perspectives to enhance our understanding of children's experiences of learning activities, their perceptions of good teachers, experiences with language learning, choral learning and various learning strategies.

"A child's life is like a piece of paper on which every passer-by leaves a mark." By understanding children's viewpoints we improve our teaching and enhance our mediation of learning and thinking processes. We are not just preparing our children for the future. When we work with children we are in many ways creating the future.

My heartiest congratulations to Ai-girl and her team for this excellent work!

Oon-seng Tan
Associate Professor
Head, Psychological Studies, National Institute of Education
Director, Singapore Centre for Teaching Thinking
President, Educational Research Association of Singapore

Preface

"Er tong shi guojia wei lai de zuren weng. Er tong shi guojia de dong liang." (Children are future leaders of the nation. Children are the nation's pillars).

CHILDREN ARE OUR FUTURE

Our future lies in positive growth of children. Children form a large proportion of human population in the world. According to the Global Population Profile (2002), children (0–14 years of age) made up 29 per cent of the world's population. Youth (15–29 years of age) and women of childbearing age (15–49 years of age) made up 64 per cent of the total. The World Population Prospects (2002) projected that for the year 2005 children (0–14 years old) would make up between 27.5 (low variant) or 28.2 (medium variant) per cent of the Asian population. Youth (15–24 years of age) would make up 18.1 (low variant) or 18.3 (medium variant) and women of childbearing age (15–49 years of age) would make up 27.4 (low variant) or 27.6 (medium variant) per cent of the total Asian population. If we take children as people whose age 18 years and below, that could mean that this group includes at least half of the world's population.

In the nineties, there were intensive efforts to improve the world's education and health. Education for all and health for all were advocated. Accordingly, in 1990, education for all was the key theme in the World Conference on Education held in Jomtien, Thailand. This world conference kicked off subsequent series of meetings (e.g., in 1993 in Delhi, in 1996 in Amman Jordan, in 2000 in Dakar, and in 2003 in New Delhi) that addressed the following issues:

- Expansion of early childhood care and developmental activities
- Universal access to and completion of basic education
- Reduction of the adult illiteracy rate
- Improvement of learning achievement
- Expansion of provision of basic education and training in other essential skills
- Knowledge, skills and values required for better living and sound and sustainable development

The international community of nations explicitly recognised that education, especially primary schooling, is critical for achieving social and demographic progress, sustained economic development and gender equality. The same intent was addressed in the Millennium Summit in 2002 and the special session of the General Assembly on children (2002). The United Nations Millennium Declaration released two key objectives: Achieving universal primary education and eliminating gender disparity. By the year 2005, gender gap in primary and secondary schools should be eliminated; and by the year 2015 universal access to primary education (education for all) should be attained (United Nation, 2003).

Likewise, for health, the World Summit on Sustainable Development (WSSD) in Johannesburg, South Africa (August 26 to September 4, 2002) inaugurated the Healthy Environment for Children Alliance (HECA). The HECA is a new, worldwide alliance to intensify global action on environmental risks to children's health. The World Health Day on April 7, 2003 was dedicated to the theme 'Healthy Environments for Children' with a call "Shaping the future of life." It is aware that more than five million children die each year from environment-related diseases and conditions such as diarrhoea, respiratory illnesses, malaria and unintentional injuries. Millions more children are debilitated by these diseases or live with chronic conditions linked to their environment, ranging from allergies to mental and physical disability. The World Health Day under the theme healthy environments for children made a stand that every child has the right to grow up in a healthy environment—to live, learn and play in healthy places. Acting to safeguard children's environments can save millions of lives, reduce diseases and provide a safer, healthier world for our children's future.

The World Health Report 2003 (Shaping the future) highlighted a close connection between health and core values of justice and security. Health is understood as "a state of complete physical, mental and social well-being." (The World Health Report, 2003: 7). Better health is a prerequisite and a major contributor to economic growth and social cohesion. New concept of health and development includes a fuller notion of human well being.

Specifically, the World Health Report 2003 elicits inequality in children's health care in different parts of the world. The contrast was seen in the following lines for two babies born in Japan and Sierra Leone. The life expectancy and health supports are rather different for the two babies, even thought they are born in the same year.

"While a baby girl born in Japan today can expect to live for about 85 years, a girl born at the same moment in Sierra Leone has a life expectancy of 36 years. The Japanese child will receive vaccinations, adequate nutrition and good schooling. If she becomes a mother she will benefit from high-quality maternity care. ... Meanwhile, the girl in Sierra Leone has little chance of receiving immunisations and a high probability of being underweight throughout childhood. She will probably marry in adolescence and go on to give birth to six or more children without assistance of a trained birth attendant. One or more of her babies will die in infancy, and she herself will be at high risk of death in childbirth." (The World Health Report, 2003: 5)

We shall seriously reflect upon the two different living conditions and pose a question: How can young girls living in places like Sierra Leone be given the same chances for a healthy life as girls born in places like Japan? (Adapted from the World Health Report, 2003: 6)

The scenario and other indicators (e.g., poverty, institutional stability and the state of basic infrastructure) give rise to serious consideration. How can we ensure that our future leaders, i.e., all today's children are given ample care and safety to grow healthily, to gain adequate education, and to participate developmentally in socio-cultural activities?

CHILDREN ARE THE WORLD'S PARTICIPANTS

Referring to the world educators' efforts in ensuring children's rights to education, health and training, one may feel amazed at the continuous momentum of the past one decade of Education for All (EFA) programmes. The World Declaration on Education for All adopted at Jomtien Thailand spoke for universal access to education as a fundamental right of all people, for fair and equitable treatment of all learners (i.e., infants, children, youth and adults). It underlined the need for better learning environments, for new partnerships, and for improved quality in educational procedures and results. The movement of EFA affirms the right of all people to basic education, people's needs and responsibilities as learners: society's expectations and requirements of its members as learners, the need for commitment, leadership and change in the educational environment and wider context to foster and facilitate learning. To ensure that contemporary societies provide stimulating and caring environments for children to grow, the convention on the rights of the child drafted on November 20, 1989 entered into force on September 2, 1990 after being ratified by 20 states. Children's rights encompass legal, psychological, sociological, policy and child advocate (see also Pardeck, 2002). Among other points, children have rights to life; freedom of expression; freedom of thought, conscience and religion; and freedom of association. The state should protect the child from all forms of maltreatment by parents or others responsible for the care of the child.

To evaluate if the effort has met the needs of children, the World EFA forum in Dakar's Senegal presented a document entitled "Global Synthesis: Education for All 2000 Assessment" (UNESCO, 2000). Issues discussed in the document included among others the scope of basic education and literacy, knowledge base, and information and communication technologies. The gender disparity has decreased in many countries. To achieve the target in 2005, a call to keep the effort abreast was reiterated in the recent meeting in New Delhi (UNESCO, 2004) to ensure equal gender opportunities to attend school, in the learning process, of learning outcomes, and of job opportunities and earnings. Gender mainstreaming, a process in bringing in what can be seen as marginal into core business for men and women, is advocated by a five-year focal framework (2002–2007) to attain parity of men and women in decision making structures, partnership, and social justice (UNESCO, 2003).

Our collective belief of children as socio-cultural torches signifies our hope for children as future leaders. This belief is indeed distinct for children in the twenty-first century who experience an increased longevity, rapid technological changes and globalisation (i.e., the interconnection of the world as a market of ideas, technology and labour, after Baltes & Freund, 2003: 26). It seems that the modern world demands children to attain higher levels of functioning or adaptive capacity (i.e., growth), to maintain the level of functioning in the face of a new challenge, and to regulate loss (Baltes et al, 1999). If such an expectation is "real", to fulfil the challenging role in the globalised world, children need to be nurtured, encouraged, supported, and engaged appropriately in everyday activities. To function optimally, children and adults alike should develop *balanced* wisdom to regulate a general-purpose mechanism—selection (directing resources and guiding behaviour), optimisation (acquiring relevant means/resources), and compensation (the uses of alternative means) (Baltes &

Freund, 2003). Children should be supported to learn to address their aspirations and needs in enriched learning environments with sufficient guidance, resources, and respect.

CONCLUDING REMARKS

Children are indeed our future and the world's participants. Affirming this statement, we have embarked on eliciting children's views in the Singapore's learning contexts.

Singapore is one of the affluent societies in East Asia and the Pacific. Since its independence in 1965, Singapore has taken education, health care and human resource development as key areas of national development. According to the statistics of year 2002, the life expectancy at birth was 80.6 years for female residents and 76.8 years for male residents. In general, Singapore has achieved gender parity in educational enrolment. The year 2003 statistics (Ministry of Education, 2004) revealed that the net enrolment rates of primary (age: 6–11 years) and secondary (age: 12–15 years) schools for year 2003 were 94 per cent and 95 per cent. The net entry rates for university and other tertiary educational institutions of the same year were 39.9 per cent and 22.4 per cent. The school expectancy for year 2003 was 12.7 years. Gender parity displayed in education and educational service enrolment. Nearly half of students in schools in year 2003 were female: elementary (48.2 per cent from n = 299,939), secondary (48.1 per cent from n = 206,426). So were polytechnic graduates (female, 48.4 per cent from n = 15,404) and university graduates (50.4 per cent from n = 10,010). Two thirds to three fourths of the teaching force of the same year were female teachers (73.5 per cent from n = 24,914), vice-principals (66.8 per cent from n = 310) and principals (63.5 per cent from n = 375). Gender disparity surfaced in the areas of specialisation. From the statistics of university graduates of year 2003, for instance, female graduates dominated moderately in the following areas of specialisation: accounting (70.2 per cent from n = 746), arts (71.7 per cent from n = 2,007), business (70.9 per cent from n = 693) and science (65.7 per cent from n = 1,190); and slightly in design and environment (55.2 per cent from n = 364) and law (57.9 per cent from n = 140). They were less represented in other areas of specialisation: Computing (33.2 per cent from n = 980), medicine (34 per cent from n = 194), dentistry (34.4 per cent from n = 32) and engineering (26.3 per cent from n = 3,317). The same trends were observed in polytechnics and institutes of technical education.

We adopt the positive spirit and compassionate wisdom of EFA. We claim that studying children's views or perceptions is indispensable, as children's views entail invaluable contextual and personal information of their experiences. Their views, for instance, may inform us of what they like or dislike and of what they deem important or unimportant. Children views can be seen as "capital materials" for teachers to work on, when necessary, to build relevance between content knowledge and children's experiences. Apart from rich and experiential information entailed in children's conceptions, espousing children's views has additional advantages, especially before and after teaching and learning. We believe that when children are invited to espouse their views, they are engaged in or tuned to, and are likely to take charge of learning. Before learning, children's perceptions are useful information for teachers to find out if their views of a phenomenon are consistent or inconsistent, correct or mis-conceptualised, as well as what their prior experiences, knowledge, preference, difficulties, and competence are. After learning, uncovering children's views can be served as a means to espouse feedback and evidence of learning.

We witnessed before the turn of the twenty-first century that Singapore's education undertook a series of curricular innovations and related infrastructure developments. The changes included expansion in physical spaces of learning in the classroom, installation of information and communication technologies for multimedia-based learning, large scale recruitment of graduate teachers, revision of teacher salaries and promotion opportunities, curricular diversity, and research on pedagogies and classroom practices. All children and teachers of the twenty-first century regardless of backgrounds are expected not only to acquire but also to create knowledge. Such changes may to a certain extent stimulate changes in classroom cultures, as well as in children's experiences in learning. Our book to a certain extent captures some of these changes.

Ai-girl Tan
April 2004

Introduction

In compiling this book, we revisited questions we posed recursively when we conducted our field and classroom research: who is a child? What are children's needs? How can we construct and co-construct stimulating learning environments for and with children? We reckoned the complexity of the subject matter, and the intensity to deliver appropriate answers to any one of these questions. To resolve our tension we intentionally took refuge in the remarks, views and verses of eminent researchers and scientists. We were pleased to note occurrences of a prefix "multi" in research and theoretical papers. For instance, the prefix "multi" is used to highlight complexity of a field or a phenomenon. Human development is multi-directional and the field of development is not homogenous but multidisciplinary (e.g., Baltes, 1987). The prefix "multi" generates innovative terms such as multi-method (to understand developmental phenomenon in a deeper sense), multi-age (how a phenomenon develops across various ages or stages of the life course) and multi-culture (how the phenomenon manifests itself in different societal settings) (Bornstein, 2002). Indeed, man is a *"unitas multiplex"* (Thomas Aquinas in Frankl, 1969/1988) or "unity in spite of multiplicity" (Frankl, 1969/1988: 22).

In this chapter, we briefly present our conceptions of a child, his/her needs, and some considerations of constructing or co-constructing stimulating learning environments for children. We also present different methods of research a teacher or a researcher can adopt to uncover children's views or perceptions of learning. The individual chapters of this book will discuss theoretical and methodological approaches pertaining to the aims of the studies.

THE CHILD

George L. Engel (1913–1999) in advancing medical and health care services advocates a bio-psycho-social model or a holistic model of care (Engel, 1977). In this model, a person is an open system interrelated with other sub-systems (i.e., physiological, psychological, and socio-cultural). In these multiple sub-systems, care for the person at the level of person (not molecular, neurological, organic or the like) is the core and fundamental consideration. The bio-psycho-social model of care echoes the inter-disciplinary care framework of palliative medicine and hospice care. A care-receiver is only part of a unit of care. Together with his/her loved ones or family, he/she forms the unit of care. Hence, a person is not an isolated but an integrated, interdependent and multifaceted being. He/she is inseparable from his/her socio-cultural networks (e.g., family and community). His/her survival and well being is dependent and interdependent on healthy relationships he/she has with these networks. It is clear that why John Bowbly (1907–1990) believed that dependency is a valuable human trait (Bowbly, 1969; Bowbly, 1973; Bowbly, 1980) and why some cultures (e.g., East Asian) place collectivist behaviour before individualistic behaviour. We learn that attachment (Ainsworth, 1969) tie infants to caregivers. And *amae* (in Japanese) facilitates intimate relatedness to other people (Doi, 1973). Humans are indeed socio-cultural beings. So are children socio-cultural participants.

Dewey (1884: 57) conceptualises a child as a person who is born into "an organized social life ... from which he/she draws his/her mental and spiritual substance, and in which he/she must perform his/her proper function or become a mental and moral wreck" (added gender pronounces). Every child possesses his/her history of development. He/she is self-determined and self-regulatory, on the one hand. His/her experience is intrinsically social and cultural, on the other hand. The three systems model conceptualises interactive relations between the person, culture, and social institutions as three interdependent systems (Csikszentmihalyi, 1988). "Each is a system because each is an organized and dynamic (i.e., moving or changing) complexity." (Much, 1995: 100) Accordingly, as a system a child is open to interactions with other systems. The child accumulates experiences through various forms of interactions with his/her surroundings, people, and objects. He/she unfolds his/her potentials independently and/or with support and guidance of adults. The psychology of a child is thus social and biological. The child learns to live with other people through socialisation, enculturation and acculturation. He/she develops his/her mind, cultivates his/her behaviour, regulates his/her emotions and feelings, and appropriates him/herself to the socio-cultural world in which he/she grows up. Bronfenbrenner's (1979) ecological conceptualisation of human development delineates another perceptive of interrelatedness of a child with his/her social systems. To sum up, children are participants, co-inhabitants, partners, successors, and future leaders. They receive sustainable socio-cultural elements and variations passed down to them across generations through verbal and non-verbal representations, as well as through socio-cultural activities and interactions.

NEEDS

Referring to Maslow's (1943) framework, a child's needs include survival, security, love and belonging, esteem, and self-actualisation. When a child is born, he/she is ready, to a great extent, to participate in social activities. Given ample support, guidance and security, infants can actively contribute to their own brain development. A newborn's brain contains about 100 billion nerve cells, or neurons, and throughout the first year of life, trillions more connections, or synapses, between these nerve cells are produced. As soon as axons make their connections, nerves begin to fire off messages: The brain is learning to communicate with itself (Honig, 1999)! Many systems of the brain contribute to one function. Early in life, neural connections or synapses form rapidly in the brain. Enriched environments have a pronounced effect on brain development during early years (Bruner, 1998).

The child's mind is plastic, and in that plasticity lies the possibility of many different ends being realised: some good and desirable, others bad and undesirable. The critical mind is attuned to observation and experiment. As psychology is a tool to reconstruct values, education is a reconstruction or reorganisation of experience which adds to the meaning of experience, and which increases the ability to direct the course of subsequent experience (Cahan, 1992; Dewey, 1913). In this manner, children can be regarded as "theorists." They conceptualise their world of knowledge through experience and socio-cultural interactions. During infancy, they begin to be aware of human intention and goal-directedness of human actions. In post-infancy, children develop an understanding of visual perception, attention, desires, emotions, intentions, beliefs, knowledge, pretence and thinking (Flavell, 1999).

Human development is evolutionary and ontogenetic (Baltes, 1997). That means, development is not completely determined by genes or by experience (see von Bertalanffy, 1933/1962). Human development can be seen as "processes that enlarge people's choices to enable them to achieve capacities (for example, the freedom to choose a healthy lifestyle, e.g., Sen, 2001)." Development is conceptualised as the natural and the cultural; and environment as a source of development. Higher mental functions depend on mastery of cultural tools. The child's potential zone of development can be expanded if he/she learns from an experienced person. The child's learning can be facilitated through scaffolding, modelling and guided discovery. In dialogue, the child uses language as a tool to monitor his/her mental functioning (Wertsh & Tulviste, 1992). Evidently, children in the course of development are aware of social happenings. In a study on children's play after the September 11, 2001 incident, it was observed that the children adopted the role of the American and the terrorists. The researcher, Beresin (2002: 331), claims that "(p)lay and game relating to September 11 reflect children's strategies for making sense with nonsense." Play and games may help simulate socio-cultural settings that make sense to children.

CO-CONSTRUCTING STIMULATING ENVIRONMENTS

Subscribing to the notion that children are participants of teaching and learning, we wish to engage children mentally, physically, and socio-culturally in learning, in lesson delivery and development as well as in problem solving and evaluation. We believe that given the opportunity, children are likely to share with others what they think, feel, and do. With encouragement, they may voice their ideals and dreams, and present them confidently to their peers, caregivers, and teachers. We extract children's implicit theories or people's conceptions (Sternberg, 1985) and everyday understanding of a phenomenon (Furnham, 1988). Our underlying assumption is that every child regardless of background is able to express, share, and elicit his/her views of his/her social happenings and of phenomena with which he/she is familiar. Children's perceptions of learning refer to children's implicit theories, conceptions, and everyday understanding of formal and informal learning, interpersonal relations, learning activities, questioning, feedback and other experiences during socialisation, enculturation and acculturation. Stimulating learning environments are likely to be co-constructed if we are able to uncover children's wishes, desirable activities, wishful teacher characteristics, and learning experiences.

Believing it is important to understand, uncover, and integrate children's perceptions of learning, we initiated a project on children's views and learning. By children, we mean students below 18 years old. We use the term "perceptions" interchangeably with views and sometimes with conceptions. Learning is a life-long activity. In all phases of development, we learn to be a better person. Hence, learning or a change in behaviour, cognition, emotion, and human relations takes place in formal and informal settings. It encompasses acquisition of skills and knowledge, finding out problems and solving them, and constructing or designing meaningful tools and activities. As such, learning spaces can be physical such as in the classroom and field, interpersonal such as in group or project work, and psychological such as in doing mental sums and dealing with emotions.

Our participants of the study included primary and secondary school students in Singapore. Upon return from graduate studies, as a young faculty member, the author conducted and designed courses on child psychology, thinking and creativity at the National Institute of Education (NIE). To have contextual understanding of what these new programmes meant to teachers and children, the author adopted indigenous, cultural, and open-ended approaches to eliciting course participants and children's views of learning and thinking. The project took off with the involvement of a schoolteacher, in collecting data on "a good teacher and a creative teacher" from the primary school children; and an experienced teacher in an interview on characteristics of caring teachers. At that time, Singapore's Education Ministry initiated new programmes to encourage nurturing of independent problem solvers, critical thinkers and creative people. Some course participants who attended the thinking and creativity modules took part in the study on "children's views on learning activities."

A Masters candidate agreed to embark on research on characteristics of teachers. We analysed responses of children and teachers to open-ended questions on qualities of a good and creative teacher. Referring to their responses and contemporary literature, we designed a survey on teacher characteristics. Another Masters candidate, interested in researching useful learning activities, based on her observations and student feedback, designed a study on secondary school students' perceptions of choral learning. A PhD candidate conducted a study on creative learning environments for the elementary school English language. In the classroom-based study, she elicited children's views on desirable activities and activities useful to motivate and engage them in learning.

Classroom action research can be conducted during teaching practice. Depending on the competence level and readiness of the teachers, innovative and creative teaching strategies can be introduced. Change takes place in the classroom when the teacher changes (Ritchie

& Rigano, 2002). We documented a teacher's intensive and innovative interactions with the primary school children. We learn that our physiology and brain mechanisms underlie affective influences on human reasoning (Le Doux, 1996). Understanding children's feelings is as indispensable as uncovering children's thinking. Feeling is a source of information in making a judgement directly, or by influencing what comes to mind (indirectly) (Schwarz, 1998). To uncover children's feelings, we can ask children simple questions such as, how do you feel about an event, a person, or an experience? Children engage in evaluative judgement of their affective reactions (e.g., feeling of liking) and their current feelings that may indeed be elicited by the target.

MULTIPLE METHODS

We believe that in supportive socio-cultural contexts organisms can contribute to their own learning. Human learning is thus unique for every individual. The uniqueness of every individual's growth and learning may induce diversified and multiple perspectives of human development. Accordingly, human learning, intelligence, and other attributes are multifarious in nature. This calls for the awareness of the researchers to take multiple perspectives into consideration when they study human learning, behaviour and cognition.

Embracing Multiplicity

In his paper entitled "Celebrating divergence: Piaget and Vygotsky," Jerome Bruner (1997) expressed his gratefulness to two giants of human development, Jean Piaget (1896–1980) and Lev Vygotsky (1896–1935) and to our good fortune to be their students. In Bruner's words, Piaget and Vygotsky taught us not to simplify. They inspired us with their intellectual power and spirit, courage and willingness to stand up to and to admit the baffling complexity of the growing mind. Growing up in different socio-political contexts, Piaget (on the edges of Neuchatelois Protestant theology) and Vygotsky (on the cultural behaviour of Russian, Jewish, Marxist literacy) conceptualised the growing minds from deep, profound and different perspectives. "Piaget was principally (though not entirely) preoccupied with the ontogenesis of *causal explanation* and its *logical and empirical justification*. ... Vygotsky ... was principally (though not entirely) concerned with the ontogenesis of *interpretation* and *understanding.*" (Bruner, 1997: 72, italics in origin) Bruner endorses positive and open reception of scientific inquiries into the same subject matter using varied methodologies and different theorisation. He synthesizes the great work of Piaget and Vygotky with insightful remarks: "Depth demands disparity." (Bruner, 1997: 72) "The opposite of great truths may also be true." (Bruner, 1997: 65) Accordingly, to embrace multiplicity of a phenomenon, we have adopted different approaches, methodologies and disciplinary expertise. A suggestion is to take the phenomenon as the core issue of investigation (Sternberg & Grigorenko, 2001), and employ multi-approaches and methods flexibly and appropriately. Another suggestion is that to take the ethics of care as the principle guide to appropriate research methodologies.

Engaging Action Researchers or Graduate Researchers

We take the stand that action researchers and graduate students should be encouraged to read a wide range of research methodologies, to ask diverse questions, and to answer these questions with reference to sound methodologies. Graduate teachers and action researchers should be able to differentiate a quantitative question (e.g., how many pages did a student read under a set of conditions) from a qualitative question (e.g., how did students interact while reading in a specific environment?). Also, it is important for them to identify the core goal of an experimental design (i.e., generation of theory by collecting data under a set of controlled, manipulated conditions) and observational design (i.e., of theory by observation in naturalistic settings)? They should know that in an experimental design, there are two conditions of study, namely, the experimental and the control. A researcher controls the relevant variables and manipulates those of interest. The research can lead to causal formulation. In an observational design, the researcher does not interfere with the context in which observations are being made (Kamil, 2004).

Qualitative methods can access personal experience and meaning, cultural diversity, contextual factors, theory or hypothesis, generation and elaboration, rare cases or conditions, and exploration of a topic in depth. They are useful tools for inquiry (Kid, 2002). They can be used for exploratory (i.e., to investigate little-understood phenomena and to identify important construct) and for explanatory (i.e., to explain the relationships between the phenomena in question, and to identify a causal or process model) studies. Examples of research methods are such as grounded theory analysis, deconstruction, discourse analysis, critical theory analysis, ethnography, feminist-based approaches, and action research and insider-outsider research (Walsh, 2003). Some of the guiding research questions include the following (Marshall & Rossman, 1989): What is happening? What are the salient themes and patterns that emerge in participants' meaning structure? How are these patterns linked? What events, beliefs and attitudes are shaping this phenomenon? How do these forces interact?

The following elicits three qualitative methods.

Diary methods (Bolger et al, 2003) examines the reported events and experiences in their natural, spontaneous context, providing information complementary to that obtainable by more traditional designs. The effectiveness of diary study designs depends on careful consideration of the question(s) one seeks to answer. Three broad types of research goals are obtaining reliable person-level information, obtaining estimates of within-person change over time as well as individual differences in such change, and conducting a causal analysis of within-person and individual differences in these changes. Questions can be: What is typical for this person with regard to a certain behaviour? How much does it different from the other with regard to this aspect? What is the source of between person differences in this aspect?

Narrative analysis (Franzosi, 1998) investigates story, plot or organisations of the events (text and narrating or narration).

In discourse analysis (Lewis, 1995), it is important to establish the flow of conversation and a feeling of involvement and coherence. Also essential is to elicit unconscious conversational styles and culturally influenced rules, norms and expectations of how a conversation should proceed. Discourse analysis looks at personal and impersonal topics. It examines paralinguistic features such as loudness, pitch, pauses, voice quality and tone.

One way to generate a research question is to sit and watch, accumulate knowledge, and conceptualise the matter. Once, the research question is set, a researcher can then conduct experimental work, and obtains results from the experiment. Next, he/she can test reliability of the results in new settings. Promising areas for experimental quantitative research are such as eye movement and reading research, neuro-psychology and reading, and readability of texts. Modern technology has made quantitative data collection and analysis for such research possible. Large scale research for making policy often is interested in finding out which method gives better results (Kamil, 2004).

There are true (randomised) and quasi (when random assignment is not possible) experimental designs (Lomax, 2004). In general, the experimental research uses univariate and bivariate for one or two variables. Multivariate methods enable more variables to be studied in a setting. The use of MANOVA (multivariate analysis) is meant for multiple dependent or outcome variables. SEM (structural equation models) involves the use of latent variables—to assess measurement error and subsequently take it into account in the analysis. It can also be used for longitudinal studies. Univariate and bivariate analyses are good for exploratory and for analytical precursors to sophisticated procedures. Group means as descriptive tools lead up to inferential tests of means such as analysis of variance. For non-experimental research, the SEM is used to test a theoretical model with a single group. Multiple linear regression (MLR) is for the prediction of a single dependent variable by multiple independent variables. Other tools for correlational analysis include factor analysis, cluster analysis, multidimensional scaling, multiple regression, path analysis, and structural equation models (Simonton, 2003).

ORGANISATION OF THE BOOK

The book is organised into five chapters. In each chapter, different methodologies are used. All chapters report action researchers' engagement in designing the studies.

In Chapter 1 we studied children's perceptions of desirable learning activities. In total, more than three hundred children took part in the studies. Adopting qualitative and quantitative methods, we uncovered primary school children's likeable activities using an open-ended question and a questionnaire developed from the responses of the children to the open-ended question and from teacher classroom observations. We employed factor, cluster, and discriminant analyses to find out the general response patterns of the children. In interpreting the responses, we also referred to our experiences with children in the classroom.

In Chapter 2 we uncovered children's perceptions of characteristics of a good teacher. Combined qualitative and quantitative methods were employed (see also Chapter 1) to develop a questionnaire. Referred to were literature reviews on characteristics of creative persons and teachers, as teachers in the twenty-first century are expected to be creative. About three hundreds children participated in the studies. We analysed the data using factor, cluster and discriminant analyses, and also interpreted differences across gender groups.

In Chapter 3 we record our teaching experiences in the English language classroom incorporating what we learned from our previous research outcomes (see Chapters 1 and 2). A total of 77 primary five pupils took part in an action research based study for a period of ten months. The study included uncovering children's desirable activities, their conceptions of creativity, and their English language performance in an innovative learning environment.

In Chapter 4 we explored 122 secondary school students' perceptions of the choral learning environment. A survey questionnaire was developed taking into consideration the responses of a pilot study in which students were requested to list what they liked and disliked about the choir. The participants rated their degree of agreement on a five-point scale on psychosocial and other perspectives of choral learning. Three research questions were posed: (1) What are Singaporean secondary school students' perceptions of choral learning? (2) Are there gender differences in their perceptions of choral learning? (3) Are there any across school differences in their perceptions of choral learning? The findings of the study were discussed from the perspectives of Singapore's education and learning environment research.

In Chapter 5 we report on innovative strategies to elicit children's views and integrate them into learning. A classroom action research study was conducted to document three best strategies a teacher designed and used to engage elementary school children into reflective and self-motivated learning. The three strategies were group brainstorming, the 3-2-1 strategy and challenge corner. In one lesson, one or more strategies can be used. The 3-2-1 strategy refers to three (3) main learning points, two (2) motivating points, and one (1) question related to the contents. This strategy can be modified according to the learning intent of a lesson. Challenge corner was meant to enable children to undertake the role of a 'teacher' to set quiz questions for their peer.

CONCLUDING REMARKS

Good research on human optimal functioning begins with precise questions, relevant perspectives and plausible methods. The research paradigm we propose in this book is multiple in nature. That means multi-dimensionality in aspects, multi-directionality in development, and multiple methods in research. Quantitative paradigms seek to ensure the adequacy of information gathering in a number of ways (e.g., standardised tests, repeated probes, or sampling intervals), which often supply reliable assessment in which they replicated. Qualitative paradigms seek to ensure adequacy of data collection by achieving saturation, i.e., when additional data collection does not add any new information. "Qualitative methods involve gathering, analyzing, and interpreting various kinds of data about individuals, groups, objects, or other entities in the contexts in which they naturally function." (Briton & Fujiki, 2003: 166) Qualitative researchers often enter the context they wish to study. They do not manipulate contexts or initiate probes. Such naturalist data collection is important to determine how children realise intervention targets in actual communication contexts, in the playgrounds and in the classrooms. There are advantages of qualitative and quantitative data. While qualitative data explain the idiosyncratic behaviour, and quantitative data allow co-relational analysis (Simonton, 2003). Quantitative methods identify cause, whereas qualitative methods search for explanation (or why) of a phenomenon under investigation (Briton & Fujiki, 2003). Adopting Frankl's (1969/1988) concern about how to attain, maintain, and restore a unified concept (of man, in our case children's views of learning) in the face of the scattered data, facts, and findings. According to him, unity (of man or in our case children's views of learning) must be sought in a more inclusive and encompassing dimension, where we can rise above ourselves to judge, evaluate and reflect upon our own deeds in moral and ethical terms (Frankl, 1969/1988). As researchers, we must know when and how to rise above the proposed and adopted methodologies of exploring children's perceptions to the level of care for children's full development. As such, studies on children's perceptions and experiences have to flexibly include relevant methodologies and frameworks as well as ethical and meaningful reflections that guide good practices and full human growth.

CHAPTER 1

Children's Perceptions of Learning Activities

INTRODUCTION

"Teaching, in a word, is inevitably based on notions about the nature of the learner's mind." (Bruner, 1997: 46)

This chapter reports on our attempt to uncover children's minds from the perspectives of learning activities they like and desire to have. In the contemporary everyday classroom, children engage in learning through various *activity structures*. Following Halliday's (1979) model of language as a semiotic resource, *activity structure* is a kind of semiotic formation. An *activity structure* is a distinct pattern of actions with a beginning and an end. Activity structures are "recurring functional sequences of actions" (Lemke, 1987: 219), or "regularly repeated and socially recognisable sequences of actions" (Chapman, 2003: 195), i.e., "the routines of classroom interaction" (Chapman, 2003: 156). The *activity structure* is recognisable and repeatable, but its action types and sequences may differ from each other on different occasions. Examples of activity structures are homework review, small-group discussion, and teacher demonstration, mental arithmetic, whole-class discussion, teacher question, student answer, and teacher evaluation. Some of the activity structures are with bigger parts (e.g., whole-class discussion), while some have smaller parts (e.g., teacher question, student answer and teacher evaluation). Different sequences of action types can constitute the same activity structure. The same subject matter classrooms (e.g., mathematics) generally exhibit the same sorts of activity structures. For instance, the activity structure "worked example" can have the following action types: questioning individual students to elicit the "correct" method; writing a formula on the blackboard; or presenting numerous examples (Chapman, 2003). Another kind of semiotic formation is *thematic formulations* which mean "recurring patterns of semantic relations among the themes and concepts of a particular way of speaking about a subject" (Lemke, 1987: 219). "Discourse analysis of thematic structures considers how the language of a text is used to develop themes, and also to relate themes to each other." (Chapman, 2003: 156)

Activity

According to the activity theory, activity is a goal-directed, self-regulated, object-oriented, artifact-mediated, and socially formed system. As the basic unit of activity, the task is a logical organised system of mental and behavioural actions directed towards an ultimate task-goal. The task in activity theory is inherently a problem-solving endeavour with an underlying subjective mental representation of the task. The task can be divided into actions and further be broken down into psychological operations or acts. Examples of tasks are diagnosis and examination of a patient. Action is a relatively bounded element of activity that fulfils an intermediate, conscious, sub-goal of activity. Cognition is a system of mental actions and operations, intimately related to external actions. Actions are the result from socio-cultural development. They are facilitated by tools, which similarly possess a history and cultural context. Examples of psychological tools of activity are meaning and sign, external tools of activity presentation controls, displays, screens, instructions, diagrams and other media, and internal tools of activity conceptual models, images of the external worlds, skills, and knowledge. Actions possess semantic, syntactic and pragmatic features analogous to words. Actions may be classified according to their psychological characteristics, i.e., psychological processes such as "memorise," "detect," and "move." Examples of such descriptions are "move the chair to the corner," "memorise the sequence of the moving of the chair," and "detect the change in the force when the chair is lifted up." The first action is less precise than the other two. During training, the actions with repetitions become automatic or unconscious. The unconscious actions embedded in operations.

A goal, the cognitive and informative component of activity, is a conscious mental representation of human activity in conjunction with a motive, the energetic (conscious or unconscious) component of activity. The self-regulation mechanism organises the activity system where cognition, behaviour and motivation are integrated toward achieving a conscious goal. Activity is socially, culturally, and historically shaped. And the human mind develops from historically contextual, object-practical activity, which determines the genesis and structure of human psychology (Rubinshtein, 1935, 1959; see Bedny et al, 2001; Leont'ev 1947, 1977; see Bedny et al, 2001). Activity determines the specificity of interaction of conscious subjects (i.e., humans, who perform according to conscious goals and their embedded tasks) with the external world. The human is an agent with accumulated historical and social experience. During this interaction, human mental processes evolve, from this follows the unity of consciousness and behaviour (Bedny et al, 2001). During activity, humans create artificial objects (i.e., artifacts) that are a necessary pre-condition for the development of internal cognitive processes. Object related activity is embedded in socially determined procedures for the manipulation of objects, which is especially true for artificial objects.

Internal activity was first performed with the support of external activity, and subsequently executed internally. Internalisation is a creative process, which involves different self-regulation mechanisms. Internalisation based on the mechanism of self-regulation—is an active process of formation of internal actions and operations. Externalisation is the transition of internal mental actions into the external plane. The process of externalisation and internalisation demonstrate that mental or cognitive activity is tightly interconnected with external object-practical activity and these two types of activity must be considered in unity (Bedny et al, 2001).

Desirable Activities

Desirable learning activities refer to learning activities the learner wishes to have, enjoys, and considers useful for knowledge and skill acquisition and innovation. There are at least three "functions" of desirable activities: (1) a source of pleasant learning environment, (2) a motivational factor for learning, and (3) a reinforcer for enhancing desirable behaviours. Desired learning activities help to promote pleasant and positive learning environments. It is assumed that a positive affect is associated with increase in brain dopamine levels released in the anterior cingulated cortex, which improves cognitive flexibility and facilitates the selection of cognitive perspective (Ashby et al, 1999). A learning environment that encourages combinational plays, joy of discovery and trial and error can bring forth positive affect which in turn can enhance the unusualness of word association (Isen et al, 1985) and problem solving (Isen et al, 1987). In contrast, stress causes impaired performance. The noradrenergic system (when test anxiety is blocked) exerts a modulatory effect on cognitive flexibility in problem solving (Beverdorf et al, 1999).

The learner's self-perception in the positive affect of the activities is a motivational factor for learning (Lange & Adler, 1997). Autonomous motivation varies as a function of one's feelings of competence and self-determination. Specifically, perceived competency and self-determination positively influence autonomous motivation, which in turn has a positive impact on performance (e.g., Deci & Ryan, 1985, 1991). Desired activities are manageable and challenging. They enhance the learners' mastery behaviours and provide them the opportunity to work independently and seek out challenging tasks. The learner is likely to perceive his/her control over and responsibility for the learning processes, methods and strategies of activities that they like. When the learner believes that he/she is sufficiently competent to execute the instrumental actions that lead to achievement, he/she will be committed to the task and be motivated to achieve.

In addition to shaping pleasant and motivational learning environments, desirable learning activities can act as reinforcers. Behaviours that occur at a naturally high rate of frequency may be used to reinforce behaviour that occurs at a low rate of frequency (Premack, 1965). Joyful behaviour such as playing games has a high rate of frequency. Presenting ideas in front of the class or in a group (e.g., brainstorming) has a low rate of frequency. Accordingly, teachers can organise games (reinforcers) after learners have successfully voiced their standpoints or opinions in public.

Studies on Children's Views

Recently, the Singapore education system had made attempts to revolutionise the culture of learning in schools. Under the new educational initiatives, the physical environment of the classroom of most elementary schools has been refurbished to include audio-video and computer facilities. Students' competence in solving creative problems is to be assessed in school-based and national examinations.

Teachers are urged to innovate classroom and extracurricular activities. Active student participation and peer evaluation are expected in the everyday classroom. Singapore's elementary school education is featured by two streaming examinations: grade 4 (age: 10 years) and grade 6 (age: 12 years). It is within this peculiar learning culture that a balanced, student-centred, innovative and academic learning framework should be established. It is indispensable to uncover pupils' views of desirable learning activities, especially in the midst of the curricular and structural innovation. In view of this shift towards an individualised learning framework, we examine elementary school pupils' perceptions of desirable learning activities within the Singaporean learning context.

Our studies were based on classroom observations, dialogues with teachers and children, an open-ended question survey, followed by a structured survey and interviews. Between 1996 and 1998, the author observed the teaching of 26 student teachers in the classroom, interacted with 42 experienced teachers who coached them, and facilitated 78 pre- and post-conferencing one-to-one and/or focused group interviews after one hour lesson observations. In addition, she conducted 36-hours modules to 60 in-service teachers, and requested over three hundred student teachers who attended six to nine hourly classes on creativity activities to find out how to nurture creativity of the Singaporean children. In the classroom observations, pre- and post-conferencing interviews, she focused on eliciting learning activities that were fun, effective, and useful for the children. Taking these experiences as background information, she interacted with the children face-to-face in the classroom.

STUDY 1

Participants

A total of 270 children from six classes participated in this study with equal gender distribution. The study was conducted in August and September 1997. The age range of the children was between seven and twelve years old. The children presented their ideas in accordance to their choices of subject (e.g., mathematics and the English language).

An Instrument

After numerous classroom observations, the author (and researcher) designed an instrument called "Learning through Playing" that invited the children to write down or draw the activities they liked and wished to have. The title of the instrument entails two significant words, i.e., "learning" and "playing" that might sound "incompatible" to the children who were used to "serious" learning featured by a competitive environment of learning that highlights high achievements and good grades. To tune the children to the task, the researcher read the instructions loudly. Different words with the meaning of "play" appeared multiple times: "fun," "enjoy," "interesting," "happiness," "like," and "wish." The role of the children was clearly elicited, as a partner of learning. As partners in learning, the children's views would influence the teacher's choice of learning activities.

> "You definitely wish to attend interesting lessons that are full of fun. To help us to design activities that you will enjoy, we would like to invite you to share with us activities that have brought you happiness. Please let us know by describing or drawing activities (*as many as possible*) that you like best, and that you wish to be carried out in the classroom."

The children were encouraged to elicit more than one idea indicated by the phrase "*as many as possible*." To enable the children to write freely, ample space was allocated for them to write or draw, about half of the A4-size paper. There was no time limit for the children to attend to the task. The researcher guided the children to write down their bio-data, but left them to attend to the task independently. The task was conducted in the English language, mathematics, science and social studies lessons.

Procedure

The teachers, who agreed to be the action researchers, read through the responses of the children. They then attempted to integrate the choices of the children into their teaching, whenever appropriate. The study of teacher researchers' choices of desirable learning activities have been reported elsewhere (see Tan, 2001a; Tan, 2001b). On average the children completed the task in about 20 minutes.

The children's responses were categorised with the help of the teachers, especially when the children presented a diagram without any description. The diagram represents an activity structure that happens in everyday classrooms. Activity structures such as group discussion and teacher demonstration that occur frequently in the children's responses were identified to be included into the instrument for the quantitative study. Other salient responses are reported below.

Means of Representation

The children's responses represented what they experienced in social learning and individualised cognitive learning. Their responses revealed their competencies in writing or expressing. In general, children used short sentences, point form, a combination of pictures and sentences, and sentences to present their ideas. Some of them played with the size of the characters and/or added some symbols (see Figure 1.1 for an example).

FIGURE 1.1   The child used different sizes of characters

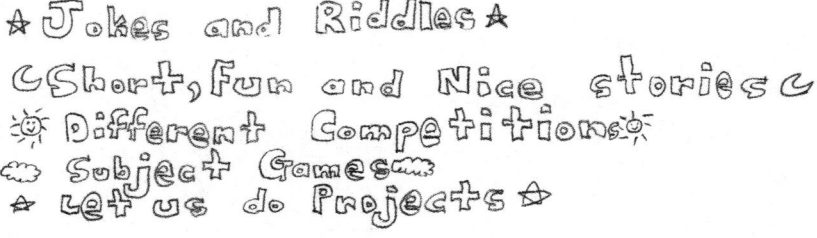

Some children combined drawing and writing (see Figure 1.2). In everyday classrooms in most group work writing, children will decorate their writing by their own drawing.

FIGURE 1.2   The child used drawing and writing to represent her desirable reading and group activities

FIGURE 1.3   The child represented her/his social context of learning in drawing

A handful of the children presented nearly all their ideas in drawing (see Figure 1.3). The drawing in Figure 1.3 informed the reader that the child constructed the desirable learning environment in a social context. Three persons in the picture represented a classmate, who says the greeting word "good-day," a learner, who questions, and a teacher, who tells a story. The picture suggests that the classmate and the learner would participate in collaborative learning. A star was placed next to the words "group work." This pictorial representation was common, for a Singaporean classroom that emphasises rewards by marking a sign "star" next to the students' or groups' name placed on a chart in the notice board.

The children listed their desirable activities according to a specific subject, such as fraction in the mathematics lessons (see Figure 1.4), as well as reading stories, acting, writing, word games, and spelling in the English language lessons (see Figure 1.5; also Figure 1.1, jokes, riddles, story, competition, games, and project).

FIGURE 1.4   The child elicited in writing his wishes for the English language lessons

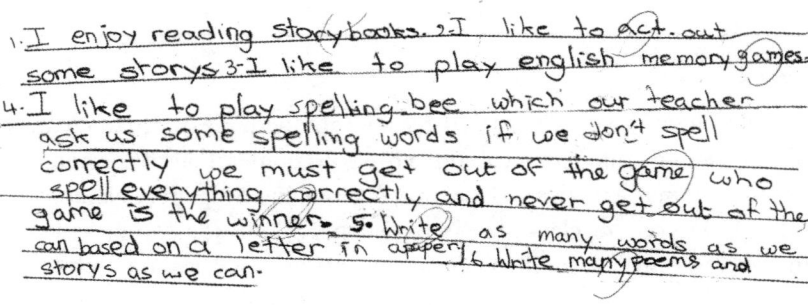

FIGURE 1.5   The child presented her wish of using pictures/drawing and writing

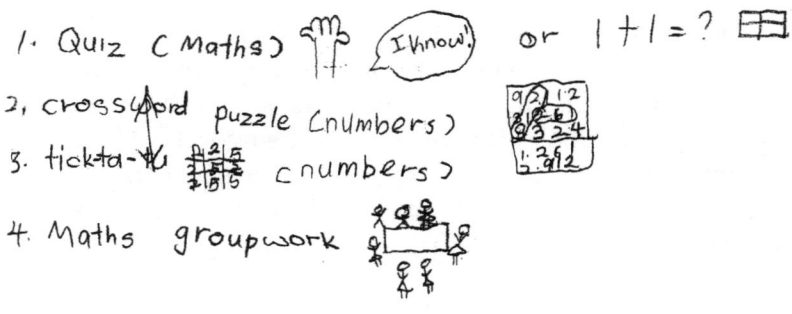

FIGURE 1.6 The child presented his favourite theme in Mathematics (fraction) in picture and words

In Figure 1.5 a child listed three desirable activities for mathematics: quiz for solving mathematical sum, crossroad numeral puzzle or numeral tic-tac, and mathematics group work. A group in a Singapore elementary school, where the class size is between 38 and 45, comprised 6–8 members. Using a combination of pictures and words, some children conveyed the procedures and structures of the activities (see Figure 1.6).

STUDY 2

The Participants

Four hundred and ten children (56.3 per cent female, 43.7 per cent male) from various Singapore elementary schools selected randomly took part in a paper-and-pencil survey. The age range of the children was 9–12 years. Nearly two-thirds of the children reported that they like learning the English language (65.4 per cent) and Mathematics (64.4 per cent). Approximately half of them like learning the mother tongue (46.8 per cent) and Science (52.2 per cent).

Formulation of Our Research Questions

Since 1997, Singaporean teachers have been encouraged to introduce innovative learning activities that can enhance pupils' critical and creative thinking and problem solving skills. They are encouraged to infuse thinking skills and strategies in lessons. The new educational initiatives challenge teachers' selection of learning activities. Interdisciplinary learning tasks and student-centred learning approaches are recommended. In view of the fact that the new educational initiatives have gradually recognised active student participation, we wish to find out Singaporean pupils' views of learning activities. Accordingly, we formulated two research questions: (1) What kinds of learning activities do children like? (2) Are there gender differences in children's perceptions of desirable learning activities?

Procedures

A questionnaire comprising thirty-three learning activities was designed with reference to responses from several exploratory studies taken part by children and teachers between 1997 and 1999. The activities included in the study were desirable learning activities (#1, 2, 3, 4, 6, 8, 9, 10, 11, 12, 13, 15, 16, 18, 19, 21, 23, 25) (Tan, 1998a; Tan, 1998b), common classroom activities (#5, 7, 14, 17, 20, 22, 24, 27, 28, 29, 31, 33) and activities that can help generate ideas (#26, 30, 32) (Tan, 1998c) (see Table 1.1 for item descriptions). The questionnaire was administered to the participants at their respective classrooms at various intervals. On average, the children completed the questionnaire within 15 minutes. They first noted their age, gender and subjects they liked. Then they rated their views of desirable activities on a 5-point-Likert scale.

To make the scale "salient" and "understandable" to the children, some techniques were used. To highlight the scale, the numbers were printed bold, and with a bigger font size, 1.5 times, than the other numbers and characters. The phrase "5-Likert scale" was not printed in the survey.

"Use the numbers 1, 2, 3, 4, 5 to indicate how much you like or dislike an activity."

Also the numbers were described with a sentence that intended to highlight the differentiated and continuous degree of likeness and personal wish. The phrases or terms that described the degree of likeness were printed in capital letters and underlined. Likewise, the word "like" was underlined. Phrases that indicated the frequency of the occurrence of an activity were placed in brackets. The sentence was bold partly to give contrasting effects and hence to make the meanings of the scale salient.

> **"If you *like* an activity *VERY MUCH* and wish to have it *ALWAYS* (in every lesson) write 5."**

Other descriptions for the scale are listed as follow:

> **"If you *like* an activity *A LOT* and wish to have it *OFTEN* (in almost every lesson) write 4."**

> **"If you *like* an activity *AVERAGE* and wish to have it *SOMETIMES* (twice a week) write 3."**

> **"If you *like* an activity *QUITE A BIT* and wish to have it *OCCASIONALLY* (once a week) write 2."**

> **"If you <u>like</u> an activity *VERY LITTLE ONLY* and wish to have it *SELDOM* (once in a month) write 1."**

The teachers who agreed to be the action researchers distributed the two-page survey to the children. They were instructed not to influence the children, but should guide the children in answering a survey and assist them in using a numeral scale to represent their wishes. It was also important to highlight to the children that there was no right or wrong response. All responses should match as closely as possible to their wishes. The children were encouraged to attend to the survey individually and independently from other children. They were allowed not to write their names on the survey. The teachers in charge would take note of their responses positively, and attempt to integrate their views in the forthcoming lessons.

Results

The Cronbach's alpha reliability of the instrument was high, at 0.90. The items were defined with regards to the findings of factor analysis, results of previous studies (Tan, 1998a, 1998b, & 1998c) and socio-educational connotations in the classroom. First, factor analysis (principal component, and oblimin with Kaiser normalisation) was computed. The analysis yielded three factors, which accounted for 40.51 per cent of the variance: F1 (24.5 per cent)–basic knowledge acquisition, F2 (11.2 per cent)–motivation, and F3 (4.8 per cent)–performance. The alpha reliabilities for the three factors were high: 0.87 for F1, 0.78 for F2, and 0.82 for F3. The range of correlation among the factors was between 0.10 and –0.43. Eigenvalue for F1 was 8.1, for F2 it was 3.7, and for F3, 1.6. The Kaiser-Meyer-Olkin Measure of Sampling Adequacy (KMO-MSA) for self-perceived teacher characteristics was high (0.89). The approximate Chi-square from the Bartlett's test of sphericity was 4783.2 (df 528) at p less than 0.0001 significant level. Next, referring to the results from previous findings, we refined the category for the purpose of this study. Activities related to basic knowledge acquisition and emphasised recall and memorisation are marked R. Learning activities that encourage collaboration are indicated by C. Activities that enhance motivation are marked M, and those that foster independent learning are recorded by I. Then we categorised the activities with reference to Weinstein's (1991) descriptions of learning activities in the classroom with special attention being paid to the Singaporean context. The letter T refers to teacher-centred activities and S to student-centred activities. Despite the efforts to categorise and define the items, we are aware that "functions" of an activity may vary according to situations such as learning objective, target group and duration. The mean and standard deviation of each item were computed for all participants and according to the subjects the children liked. The items yielded two clusters (from cluster analysis). Results of the discriminant analysis on the four factors showed that 94.7 per cent of participants were correctly classified into the three clusters. Table 1.1 summarises the descriptive statistics, factor loadings, and final cluster centres of the items.

The thirty-three items were clustered (from cluster analysis) according to the subjects the children liked. Table 1.2 shows results of the cluster analysis.

TABLE 1.1 Pupils' perceptions: Descriptive statistics, factor loadings, and final cluster centres

	Items	M	SD	Rank	%	S/T	Act	Factor loading	C1	C2
1	Games	4.28	1.05	1	59.6	S/T	M	F2	0.75	4	4
24	Rest/recess	4.23	1.31	2	66.0	S	M	F2	0.62	4	4
4	Learn computer skills	4.21	1.24	3	63.1	T	M	F2	0.41	4	4
14	Learn outside the classroom	3.97	1.51	4	59.7	S	I	F2	0.52	4	3
16	Read a book	3.92	1.39	5	49.3	S/T	C	F1	0.43	4	3
7	Listen to or tell jokes	3.88	1.34	6	47.1	T	M	F2	0.65	4	3
13	Spell words correctly	3.76	1.54	7.5	46.4	T	R	F1	0.42	4	3
2	Riddles	3.76	1.30	7.5	36.2	T	M	F2	-0.60	4	3
19	Group competition	3.72	1.69	9	53.2	S/T	C	F3	-0.44a	4	2
10	Video show	3.71	1.51	10	48.5	S/T	C	F2	0.66	4	3
21	Quiz	3.68	1.60	11	47.8	T	C	F2	0.42	3	1
15	Correct my own mistakes	3.67	1.49	12.5	41.7	T	R	F1	0.68	4	2
20	Teacher demonstration	3.67	1.45	12.5	39.1	T	R	F1	0.75	4	2
6	Solve puzzles	3.54	1.42	14	34.2	S	C	F2	0.49	4	3
18	Construct something	3.45	1.64	15	38.3	S	I	F3	-0.43	4	2
8	Group discussion	3.39	1.46	16	28.6	S	C	F3	-0.62	4	2
27	Learn grammar	3.36	1.63	17	34.1	T	R	F1	0.82	4	2
33	Solve a problem	3.35	1.64	18	35.4	S	I	F1	0.59	4	2
28	Remember multiplication tables	3.30	1.81	19	40.8	T	R	F1	0.67	4	2
11	Do worksheet	3.24	1.53	20	25.5	T	R	F1	0.74	3	2
17	Role play	3.23	1.70	21	35.4	S/T	C	F3	-0.41a	4	2

TABLE 1.1 (cont'd)

3	Listen to or tell story	3.21	1.53	22	28.6	T	M	–	–	3	2
26	Suggest new ideas	3.14	1.52	23	24.0	S	I	F3	-0.58	3	2
30	Share my ideas with classmates	3.09	1.50	24	20.6	S	C	F3	-0.45	3	2
25	Act or show and tell	3.06	1.73	25	29.6	S/T	M	F3	-0.60	3	1
31	Mental sum	3.03	1.72	26	30.6	T	R	F1	0.42	4	1
12	Do project	3.00	1.67	27	28.5	S	I	F3	-0.60	3	2
9	Ask the teacher question	2.99	1.58	28	23.3	S	I	F1	0.43	3	2
32	Write down my ideas	2.92	1.67	29	22.8	S	C	F3	-0.60	3	1
23	Write an essay/composition	2.67	1.62	30	17.5	T	R	F1	$0.43b$	3	1
22	Test/examination	2.61	1.79	31	21.8	T	R	F1	0.53	3	1
29	Remedial class/tuition	2.46	1.70	32	19.7	T	R	F1	$0.53b$	3	1
5	Present my work in front of the class	2.28	1.59	33	12.4	S	I	F3	-0.60	2	1

NOTE: N = 410

% = students' rating —'5'- very desirable

a— items with a factor loading 0.30 for F2

b— items with a factor loading 0.30 for F3

TABLE 1.2 Final cluster centres of pupils' perception of desirable learning activities according to preferred subjects

Items		English C1	English C2	Mother tongue C1	Mother tongue C2	Mathematics C1	Mathematics C2	Science C1	Science C2
1	Games	4	4	4	4	4	4	4	4
24	Rest/recess	4	4	3	4	4	4	4	4
4	Learn computer skills	4	4	3	4	4	4	4	4
14	Learn outside the classroom	4	4	3	4	4	3	4	3
16	Read a book	4	4	3	4	4	3	4	3
7	Listen to or tell jokes	4	4	3	4	4	3	4	3
13	Spell words correctly	4	3	4	4	4	3	4	3
2	Riddles	4	4	3	4	4	3	4	3
19	Group competition	4	2	1	4	4	2	4	2
10	Video show	4	4	3	4	4	3	4	3
21	Quiz	3	2	2	4	4	2	4	2
15	Correct my own mistakes	4	3	3	4	4	3	4	3
20	Teacher demonstration	4	3	3	4	4	3	4	2
6	Solve puzzles	4	3	3	4	4	3	4	2
18	Construct something	4	3	2	4	4	2	4	2
8	Group discussion	4	3	2	4	4	2	4	2
27	Learn grammar	4	2	2	4	4	2	4	2
33	Solve a problem	4	2	2	4	4	2	4	2
28	Remember multiplication tables	4	2	3	4	4	2	3	2
11	Do worksheet	4	2	2	4	4	3	4	3
17	Role play	3	3	2	3	4	2	3	1
3	Listen to or tell story	4	3	3	3	3	2	3	2
26	Suggest new ideas	4	2	2	3	4	2	4	2
30	Share my ideas with classmates	4	2	2	3	3	2	3	2
25	Act or show and tell	3	2	1	3	4	1	3	1
31	Mental sum	4	1	2	3	4	2	3	2
12	Do project	3	2	2	3	3	2	3	2
9	Ask the teacher question	3	2	2	3	3	2	3	2
32	Write down my ideas	4	1	2	3	4	2	3	1
23	Write an essay/composition	4	1	1	3	3	1	3	1
22	Test/examination	3	1	1	3	3	2	3	1
29	Remedial class/tuition	3	1	1	3	3	2	3	1
5	Present my work in front of the class	3	1	1	2	3	1	2	1

TABLE 1.3 Distance between clusters, frequency and percentage of pupils that belonged to the clusters

	Overall	English	Mother tongue	Math	Science
Distance between clusters	9.00	7.87	8.83	7.80	8.64
Percentage of children					
C1	84.6	50.0	6.6	49.0	47.1
C2	15.4	15.4	40.2	15.4	5.1
Number of children					
C1	347	205	27	201	193
C2	63	63	165	63	21
Total	410	268	192	264	214

Distance between clusters and number and percentage of children that belonged to the clusters were shown in Table 1.3.

The independent two-sample t-test was computed across gender groups according to the preferred subjects. Table 1.4 shows the range of mean and the significantly different items.

DISCUSSION

Multiple Methods

The studies used qualitative and quantitative analysis. By using an open-ended question, the researcher was able to address the "what is" component of desirable and useful learning activities. Embedded into the responses of the children was valuable information. This includes the degree of likeability, such as the use of "more" to indicate that the current state could be improved. "Tell us more about interesting stories. Challenge us with more challenging problem sums." Also included was the preferred timing or schedule of the activities: "Set quizzes twice or thrice a week." "Give us quiz or game when we have free time." The children's responses revealed the theme of learning, and displayed the significance of knowledge and skill acquisition: "I like fractions. I can

17

TABLE 1.4 Range of mean difference and results of significantly different items across gender groups according to preferred subjects

	Mean difference	Female M	Female SD	Male M	Male SD
Overall	−0.29 to 0.90				
Read a book		4.16	1.23	3.60	1.54***
Correct mistake		3.83	1.38	3.42	1.61**
Teacher demonstration		3.78	1.35	3.49	1.59*
Learn grammar		3.50	1.59	3.14	1.68*
Do worksheet		3.49	1.40	2.89	1.63***
English	−0.48 to 0.54				
Read a book		4.35	1.03	3.86	1.33**
Do worksheet		3.66	1.25	3.13	1.60**
Group discussion		3.18	1.51	3.65	1.25**
Suggest new ideas		3.06	1.53	3.43	1.39*
Mother tongue	−0.45 to 0.53				
Read a book		4.06	1.31	3.52	1.54*
Games		4.02	1.19	4.45	0.93*
Learn grammar		3.77	1.43	3.24	1.66*
Riddles		3.67	1.28	4.12	1.20*
Do worksheet		3.67	1.36	3.20	1.56*
Mathematics	−0.40 to 0.54				
Read a book		4.20	1.24	3.67	1.50**
Do worksheet		3.59	1.39	3.07	1.59**
Group discussion		3.17	1.49	3.65	1.25**
Science	−0.30 to 0.54				
Read a book		4.35	1.01	3.81	1.40**
Group discussion		3.28	1.43	3.73	1.28*

NOTE: * $p < 0.05$; ** $p < 0.001$

learn halves and quarters from fractions. I know that two halves can make one whole." This child employed the words "like" "can" and "know" to relate desirability and competency. In another example: "I like fraction because I can cut things equal," the child used "because" to relate likeability and functionality of learning fraction. Also, the children's responses reflected the nature of the learning activities, making paper shapes from a whole to parts and vice versa. In addition, the children's responses entailed their conceptions of meaningful learning. "Tell jokes when we are quiet." Jokes were perceived by the child as a form of reward for good behaviour. "If I have finished revising social studies, I would like to have spelling based on the subject." The same child suggested the sequence of two activity structures related to the subject social studies: revision and then spelling. The valuable information gathered from qualitative data supported the interpretation of the quantitative data which enabled the researcher to find out the children's main preferred common desirable and useful activities. In the quantitative analysis, the inquiry into "how many" was addressed.

We further organised our discussion according to the two research questions. The findings will be discussed within the Singaporean elementary school pupils' learning context.

Children's Desirable Activities

From the various statistical analyses, we notice that the children liked activities that are interactive and joyful (e.g., games, quizzes and riddles), familiar (e.g., reading, spelling words and competition), relaxing (e.g., resting and joking), and bring forth novel experiences (e.g., computer learning, outdoor activities and video shows). Children spend most of the instructional time (half a day) in the same classroom. Outdoor learning such as visiting a museum, historical places and the science centre is part of the elementary school curricula. The teachers organise these activities occasionally (once or twice per term). Computer learning is a new subject in schools. Children learn about computers in the resource room. Change of activities (e.g., games, group competition, listening to jokes, going for recess and learning computer skills) involves change of seating arrangements (from individual to group seating) or venues (walking to and back from the resource room or canteen) and thus creates opportunities to move and talk. In summary, the pupils' perceptions of

19

desirable activities entail the elements of joyfulness, manageability, pleasant experiences, and variability (or variation). In contrast, the children liked to a lesser degree, activities that may induce anxiety (e.g., test) and are less familiar (e.g., suggesting ideas and project work). They did not give favourable responses to activities that demand verbal performance (e.g., verbal presentation, asking question, role-play, show and tell and story telling) and writing competence (e.g., essay writing, writing down ideas). They did not indicate a high degree of desirability for repetitive activities (e.g., doing worksheet, remedial classes and mental sum). We may infer that the pupils' less desirable activities entail the connotations of boredom, fear of performing and stress from examinations.

Next, we discuss some observations pertaining to the Singaporean context. Our findings confirm results of the previous studies (see Tan, 1998a; Tan, 1998c): elementary school children do not like activities that challenge their verbal and writing competence. In Singapore, English is the main medium of instruction. Mandarin, Malay or Tamil are taught during mother tongue and moral education lessons. Pupils' bilingual development largely depends on the English language and mother tongue lessons. During the linguistic development phase, the children may be less confident in articulating their views using either one of these languages. This could be one of the reasons why the children did not rate highly these activities. Another reason could be attributed to insufficient opportunities to participate actively in these activities. Singaporean children of the upper elementary school levels are likely to spend most of the instructional time in completing the syllabi several months before the streaming examinations. Activities that demand the students to perform (e.g., verbal presentation, role-play and story telling) require more instructional time than individual seatwork (e.g., spelling, doing worksheet). Hence, the teachers are less likely to frequently organise such activities for students of the examination years.

Regardless of preferred subjects, the children did not rate highly, project work, a core activity to be introduced in the next several years. Until the research was conducted, most of the schools introduced project work during extracurricular activities. Unfamiliarity is the cause of the pupils' low rating.

Gender Diversity

Gender different preferences were observed for some activities (e.g., reading, group discussion). The female participants rated routine activities significantly higher than did their male counterparts. Many schools conduct a whole school reading exercise in the hall once a week, 20 minutes before the school day begins. Children bring their favourite books to the hall, sit on the floor and read the books in silence. Reading appeared to be a significant activity rated higher by female children than by male children across preferred subjects (English, Mathematics, mother tongue, and Science). The same findings were observed for correcting mistakes, doing worksheets, teacher demonstration and learning grammar. We may postulate that female children like to attend to routine activities or are linguistically inclined.

Children learn new responses simply by observing the behaviours of others or from modelling (see e.g., Bandura, 1978). They would be excited to interact freely with their friends and peers without strict supervision from the teacher. Our significant findings suggest that male children liked interactive activities (e.g., games and riddles). The male participants rated significantly higher than the female participants for group discussion across various preferred subjects: English, Mathematics and Science, and for all preferred subjects. The male participants who liked the mother tongue rated significantly higher than the female participants, for games and riddles. The same finding is observed for participants who liked all subjects. The male participants seemed to like suggesting new ideas more than did their female counterparts (see preferred English subject). Future studies should examine the relation between female students' linguistic competence (or male students' interpersonal competence) and their preferred activities.

Thematic Formations

Children who liked English and Mathematics did not show domain-specific preferences or thematic formations for the activities. Most Singapore elementary school teachers are qualified to teach English and Mathematics. As such, teachers may be responsible for teaching these two subjects to a class of students. Under the supervision of the same teacher, children are likely to be exposed to *similar* teaching styles and learning activities. Hence, it is likely that a less distinct domain-specific preference is observed for the two subjects. In contrast, a domain-specific preference was observed for the children who liked Science. The children who liked Science did not have high cluster centres for activities such as mental sum, show and tell, role-play and memorisation of multiplication tables. Science is taught by teachers who had graduated with this specialisation. During Science lessons, it is therefore likely for children to be exposed to *different* teaching styles and learning activities.

From the number of final cluster centres with a high rating of "4," we may infer that children who liked mother tongue had less interest in a variety of activities (C1: nact = 20, C2: nact = 3) than their counterparts who liked English (C1: nact = 24, C2: nact = 8), for instance. Children spend less instructional time to learn or use their mother tongue than they do for English, in the classroom. Furthermore, the additional role of mother tongue teachers as cultural transmitters could restrict their teaching styles, which highlights restoring societal values. Often, children of different classes whose mother tongue competence are of the same level, and are gathered for the same lesson in the mother tongue room or a classroom available during the instructional time. The children take five to ten minutes to gather themselves for the mother tongue lessons and to return to their respective classrooms. Consequently, teachers may have to have less instructional time to try using audio-video facilities or to use extra learning materials.

Suggestions for Future Studies

Using an instrument developed within the Singaporean socio-educational context, we identified activities children like (or dislike). Accordingly, we infer factors that influence pupils' learning and their preferred learning activities. Future studies should examine ways to reduce differences caused by physical and social-linguistic constraints of learning. To have a comprehensive profile of pupils' learning, the present instrument can be used together with other instruments that uncover pupils' learning motivation, stress, coping strategies, etc. Actual classroom observations should be included into the research design to find out if the preferred learning activities can increase learning performances. Future studies should also investigate how an activity is introduced to children. What kind of social connotations do children attach to an activity introduced by teachers of various teaching styles (e.g., student-centred versus teacher-centred)? Some learning activities may be a motivational factor for a certain group. Others may regard the same activities as stressful events. The "socio-educational functions" of an activity vary according to groups and situations. To enhance effective learning, it is crucial to envisage possible 'functional' roles of an activity within the same or different personal and socio-educational context at various time intervals.

Would organisation of the activity (e.g., design, assessment, duration, frequency, autonomy and expected outcomes) influence the degree of desirability and its effectiveness for learning? Effective learning activities allow learners to discover solutions for themselves to every problem in a given field through for instance, insightful questions and prompting by teachers (see e.g., Bruner, 1987). It is indispensable to examine learning activities in light of providing the learners with ample opportunities to uncover their potential and develop competence. Well-organised collaborative learning can help facilitate the development of cognitive and interpersonal strategies for information processing and problem solving. Challenging individual learning can foster the development of cognitive and intrapersonal competence.

Living in a multilingual society, the pupils' bilingual competence is crucially important for intra- and interethnic communication. Accordingly, future studies should examine if pupils' desirable learning activities influence their attitudes toward and competence in linguistic performances. Intervention programs should be established to remove negative connotations of some learning activities and to reduce the frequency of undesirable activities. Discovery learning is mainly conceptual, has relatively long lasting consequences, and promotes comparatively greater feelings of self-esteem of the learner (e.g., Deci et al, 1980). Learning activities that enhance independent thinking and interdisciplinary information exchange should be introduced step-by-step and through pupils' active participation.

Final Words

Pupils are the core group of participants of new educational programs. Accurate assessment on the effectiveness of any new educational program depends on the success of the teachers to collect representative and precise student feedback and comments. Accordingly, scientific studies on pupils' conceptions of learning and learning activities should be conducted before, during and after the implementation of a new initiative. Until educators recognise the importance of pupils' views and desirable learning activities, learning environments that bring forth positive affect would be less likely to be constructed. Unless educators and policymakers operationalise an individualised and socio-educational framework of learning, pupils' potential competence cannot be uncovered and nurtured to the fullest.

CHAPTER 2

Children's Perceptions of Teacher Characteristics: A Good Teacher

TAN AI-GIRL, RASLINDA RASIDIR AND
HONG EE-LI

INTRODUCTION

The age when the theory of mind begins is still under debate. Nonetheless, developmental psychologists (e.g., Piaget, see Astington & Barriault, 2001; Erikson, see Eccles, 1999) agree that children have a better understanding of the mind after age six. Several types of learning and understanding are featured in middle childhood. These include skills of self-awareness, increasing ability to reflect on themselves and take perspectives of others, and being a good girl (boy) (theories of development of Erikson & Kohlberg, see Miazga, 2000). Referring to the model of cognitive development proposed by Piaget, children's cognition in these age groups is relatively close to adults' thinking. Children's reasoning is flexible, organised, and logical. They can perform a variety of problems that involve operational thinking—conservation, transitivity, and hierarchical classification, as well as spatial relationships among objects (Piaget, 1962). Around grade three, children discover consistencies in the overt behaviour of people they know. They begin to describe these people in terms of motives, beliefs, abilities, interests, and attitudes (e.g., Barenboim, 1977; Livesley & Bromley, 1973; Peevers & Secord, 1973). Children of these age groups have developed their ability to imagine what other people may be thinking and feeling or the perspective taking skills (see Selmon, 1980; Selmon & Byrne, 1974). They understand the existence of the self's and the others' inner thoughts and feelings, can see their thoughts, feelings, and behaviours from another person's perspective, and recognise that others can do the same. Some of them can imagine how the self and others are viewed from a third party 'generalised other' position. Through interacting with peer and adults, children develop moral reasoning, self-control and self-responsibility. During the elementary school ages, children are able to understand good or bad behaviours (Kohlberg, 1969, 1976). Some psychologists highlight the importance of continuity in understanding human development (e.g., Bjorklund, 1999) and children's competence in handling world problems and in understanding social phenomena. They believe that children are competent social actors who have a particular perspective on the social world worth listening to (James & James, 2000).

Perception is composed of conscious psychological processes of particular material things present to sense (Williams, 1981). Children's perceptions of phenomena are useful information about their constructed worldviews, such as their interpretation of the encountered people and socio-cultural environments, and their meaning of life experiences. The social worlds, especially the immediate ones (the child's family and friends) play a vital role in children's understanding of other people's mind and behaviour. Recent studies on life-span development show that there are personality continuities from childhood to adulthood (e.g., Caspi, 2000). Over years of development children construct a relatively "stable" view of the people and their surroundings. Evidently, children possess self-assessment of competencies (Stipek & MacIver, 1998), and are able to convey their competency beliefs. By the age of 10 years old, children have developed a stable and consistent set of beliefs about themselves. Older children (above 10 years of age) are more accurate in their self-perceptions than the younger children (Bouffard et al, 1998). Children between 8 and 11 acquire various types of competencies in perceiving their social worlds and people around them. In fact, children of the age range show a pattern of brain activation in a spatial working memory task that is remarkably similar to that of adults (Nelson et. al, 2000).

GOOD TEACHER

Children possess implicit theories of a good teacher. Jules and Kutnik (1997) in their study asked pupils to write an essay on "a good teacher" based on their own classroom experiences. From the 1,539 essays, they discovered that children identified physical appearance and regular attendance as the main physical and personal characteristics of a good teacher. Children expected teachers' caring and kind dispositions. They also consistently identified teachers' ability to control and manage the class. These findings were in line with their earlier study (Kutnik & Jules, 1993) on children from Trinidad and Tobago. In addition, they discovered that younger pupils focused on appearance, subjects taught and assertion of physical punishment. Mid-aged pupils focused on the range of classroom control used by teachers, action involved in the teaching process and a growing awareness of the individual needs of pupils. The oldest pupils understood that good teachers must be well trained and highly motivated, should be sensitive and responsive to the needs of pupils, able to draw the pupils into the learning process and have a major responsibility in preparing the pupils for the world of work and further education.

Good teachers know how to build successful relationships with their pupils (Furman, 1990). Beishuizen and colleagues (2001) studied students' and teachers' views on two characteristics of good teachers, i.e., personality and ability. Their results show that primary school students and teachers disagreed about the characteristics of good teachers. The former described good teachers primarily as competent instructors, focusing on transfer of knowledge and skills. Beishuizen and colleagues (2001) reported that secondary school students emphasised relational aspects of good teachers, which were less disagreeable with the teachers' views. In another study conducted by McIntyre and Battle (1998) on pupils with emotional and behaviour disorders, four trait categories of good teachers identified were personality traits, respectful treatment of pupils, behaviour management practices and instructional skills. A good teacher should be able to facilitate a good teacher and student relation (see e.g., Bergreen, 1998).

Are good teachers creative teachers?

Cropley (1992) believed that to facilitate creativity, teachers should use special teaching and learning methods that are diffused throughout the whole curriculum. Teachers who do this are more effective in enhancing students' creative abilities than teachers who use traditional methods (Esquivel, 1995). Cropley (1997) also suggested that teachers should:

• show that they value creativity
• encourage children to try out new ideas
• encourage tolerance for "way-out" ideas
• avoid forcing pre-digested solutions onto children

27

- encourage independent thinking
- offer constructive criticism
- make time and materials available for following up children's ideas
- encourage children to be many sided in their outlook
- show that they themselves are flexible, many sided and interested in creative effort

In addition, Cropley (1992) pointed out that creative teachers provide a model of creative behaviour, reinforce such behaviour when students exhibit it and establish a classroom atmosphere that is supportive of creativity. Fryer and Collings (1991) used Torrance's Ideal Child Checklist along with a specially designed questionnaire, on a group of British teachers to examine their definitions of creativity and their preferred criteria for assessment. They found that 94 per cent of the teachers surveyed believed that a creative teacher is one way to develop creativity. Most of the teachers in the sample defined and assessed creativity in terms of imagination, originality and self-expression.

Diakidoy and Kanari (1999) examined student teachers' beliefs about creativity, found that the student teachers in their sample believe that it is possible to facilitate creativity in everyone and that it is within the power of the teacher to facilitate it in pupils. The student teachers also perceived the environment to play a critical role in the manifestation of creativity. They also shared the position adopted by Amabile and Hennesy (1987) and by Sternberg (1996) that environments, which emphasised conformity, competition and evaluation are least likely to encourage creativity.

McLeod and Cropley (1989) identified creative teachers as those who are:

- inclined to be flexible and willing to "get off the beaten track"
- resourceful in introducing new materials and finding ways to present knowledge to children
- capable of enjoying good relations with all of their students but inclined to have particularly good relations with highly divergent children
- likely to be non-conforming and even critical and fault-finding in their relationship with their colleagues
- self-critical and frequently dissatisfied with themselves and the system in which they are operating

It is likely that "no creative individual has all of the identified characteristics, but a creative person probably has more of them than does a less creative person." (Stein, 1974: 60)

Creative teaching consists of three levels (Treffinger et al, 1968). At the first level, students are taught to generalise and analyse ideas in response to teacher's instructions aimed at skill mastery. At the next level, teachers as leaders guide students through structured activities that would provide them with practice of the newly acquired skills. At the last level, teachers become facilitators, challenge students to use and apply their skills in actual problem-solving situations. Teachers need to serve as "sponsors" of creativity in the classrooms (Cropley, 1992). This involves approving divergent ideas, providing opportunities for non-evaluated activities and guiding students to evaluate their own work. Teacher attitudes are as important to the development of student creativity as teacher behaviours that reinforce it (Dacey, 1989; Torrance & Myers, 1978).

There are three modes in which people can influence other people's behaviour (Zajonc, 1965). The first mode is by modelling behaviour. Teachers influence pupils through the kinds of behaviour they display. The second mode is by "energising" learning. When the climate or atmosphere in the classroom is favourable, creativity is energised. The third mode is by administering differential reinforcement to successive approximation of the required behaviour. The teacher establishes the patterns of rewards and punishment, the kinds of behaviour that are encouraged and the activities for which opportunities are provided. In conclusion, we claim that in education for being good and creative, teachers have to be ready to adopt roles (i.e., mentor, facilitator, and creator, see Tan, 1997), behaviour, and to design instructions that elicit the desired learning outcomes. Teachers may learn to display selectively qualities or characteristics to match their strengths and needs of a specific group of children.

Our study examined children's perceptions of a good teacher. Two research questions were posed:

- What are children's perceptions of characteristics of a good teacher?
- Are there gender differences for children's perceptions of characteristics of a good teacher?

THE STUDY

Participants

A total of 320 children participated in a paper-and-pencil survey. Of the total, 157 (49.1 per cent) were female, and 163 (50.9 per cent) were male students. The children's age ranged between eight and eleven years. All children learn the English language and their mother tongue (Mandarin, Malay, or Tamil) in schools. The English language is the main medium of instruction, whereas the mother tongue is a subject and the language for moral education.

Instrument

The instrument for the study was a questionnaire developed between 1997 and 1999. In developing this questionnaire, we took into account the views of the children and the teachers. Using two twenty-sentence forms (one for characteristics of a good teacher, the other for characteristics of a creative teacher), 100 student teachers (age 20–30 years) and 80 elementary school students (age 8–12 years) listed out qualities of a creative teacher and a good teacher. Two questions were posed: (1) What are the qualities of a good teacher? (2) What are the qualities of a creative teacher? For each question, twenty blank lines were prepared. The children were allowed to write their ideas in any language they were most familiar such as the English and Malay languages, and Mandarin (the standardised Chinese language). They were encouraged to write the ideas that came to their mind, and avoid evaluating whether the ideas were sound, logical, or important. Since, there was no good or bad perception, the children were told to write down the ideas as if they would give the answer to the questions to themselves. The two researchers were bi- (the English and Malay languages) or multi-lingual (the English language, the Malay language, Mandarin and other languages). The second author examined the data and identified the most commonly appearing terms such as caring, patient, fair and just. She then counted the number of responses for each term. Synonyms were grouped together to a common term, for instance, "humour" included being funny and telling jokes and "communication skills" included being able to deliver lessons clearly, and being able to communicate with parents. We included negation to items with the same connotations but phrased in the positive manner, for instance "not boring" was grouped to "interesting," "not strict" to "friendly," and "not proud" to "polite". As far as possible, the researcher incorporated the responses to the common terms. Based on these responses, we prepared a master list. In the master list, we first considered the children's categories and items, and then we compared them with those of the student teachers. Next, we added new categories and items of the teachers' list, that is, the items different from those in the children's list, to the master list. Finally, we referred to the contemporary literature, and included categories and items that were not proposed by the participants (see below).

Categories and items from the children's responses:

- Physical attractiveness/appearance.
- Affective characteristics/personality (e.g., fair, just, patient, friendly).
- Social image (e.g., clever, smart, wise, intelligent, high score in examinations).
- Lively personality (e.g., tell jokes, funny, full of fun, humorous, enthusiastic, motivated).
- Non-academic (sport, music- arts, languages).
- Multiple talents (with various skills).
- Being able to invent, do experiment, to construct something.
- Knowledgeable, many ideas.
- Hardworking.
- Being different, with special talents, confident, fast, adventurous, think fast.
- Activity for enhancing creativity: a) outdoor, conducive environment, games, quizzes, b) encouraging, challenging, c) role modelling, and d) rewarding pupils.

Categories and items from the teachers (in addition to what the children proposed):

- Pedagogical aspect: Use of multi-media (e.g., IT, computer and video), new teaching methods, different teaching strategies, discourage rote learning, encourage pupils to think, use visual aids (charts, graphics, diagrams, cards, real life object, manipulative, etc.), group work, project work, good communicator, and clarity of voice.
- Personality: Unconventional, risk taker, open-minded (e.g., accept comment/opinion), motivated/interested in work, spontaneous/

witty/full of ideas, innovative (come out with new ideas), optimistic (always think positive), inquisitive (curiosity, asking many questions), and imaginative.

Categories and items from the literature (in addition to what the children and teachers mentioned):

- Implicit theories of a creative person (Sternberg, 1985): Examples of the items are making up rules as he/she goes along, think widely; carefree/full of fun; day dreaming; non-conformist; making connections and distinctions between ideas and things; having the ability to understand similarities and differences; being productive (come out with good quality works); being alone when creating something new; using the materials around him or her and makes something unique out of them; questioning societal norms, truisms, assumption; being motivated by goals; being energetic, being lively; being inquisitive at an early age.

- Teacher competence (McLeod & Cropley 1989; in Cropley, 1992: 81): Resourceful in introducing new materials and in finding ways to present knowledge to children; capable of enjoying good relations with all of their students; likely to be non-conforming and even critical and fault finding in their relationship with their colleagues; self-critical and frequently dissatisfied with themselves and the system in which they are operating.

After listing out the categories, we examined the semantic equivalence of the categories, namely, the comprehensiveness of the wordings. We examined the meanings of the statements from the perspectives of the target group. To make the statements comprehensive within the target group's learning context, we adopted several strategies. First, we examined if the statement was ambiguous or it contained unclear messages. For instance, we omitted the figurative explanation for having fun "has a free spirit—a ghost!" or day dreaming "builds castles in the sky" (Sternberg, 1985). Next, we modified some phrases found in the literature by proposing supplementary phrases. For instance, making up rules as he/she goes along, think widely (Sternberg, 1985), we proposed "try to do what others think is not possible, experimenting new ideas, tends not to know own limitations." In another example, we explained non-conformist using the terms "unconventional, do not follow norms/ old methods". Furthermore, we rephrased some expressions with words that are more familiar to our target group. An example was "follows her/ his gut feelings," we replaced with "follows her or his wills." Finally, we examined the meanings of the fifty-nine items of the master list.

Procedures

The questionnaire was distributed to the children in their classrooms by the second author at different time intervals between February 2000 and April 2000. The children were requested to read all the characteristics, and rate them according to the degree of importance on a 5-point Likert scale. Number "1" referred to "not important at all," and number "5" denoted "very important." To avoid ambiguity, descriptors were added for number "4" (important), "3" (moderately important), and "2" (not that important). They rated characteristics of a good teacher. To ensure that the participants understood the contents and the techniques of answering, the researcher read the instructions and the list of characteristics before the children attended to the questionnaire individually. All the items were presented in the English language. The average time to complete the questionnaire was thirty minutes.

RESULTS

The Cronbach's alpha reliability for the children's ratings on the fifty-nine items for a good teacher was high; 0.93. Mean and standard deviation for characteristics of a good teacher were computed. Cluster analysis on the responses for the fifty-nine items of characteristics of a good teacher yielded three clusters. The distance between Cluster 1 (C1) and Cluster 2 (C2) was 10.6, between C1 and C3 (cluster 3) was 4.3, and between C2 and C3 was 8.5. The cluster C1 was featured by only one item (#28, hard working), with a value of the final cluster centre 5. There was a total of 37 (11.6 per cent) of the participants belonged to this cluster. The cluster C2 was featured by 15 items, which was composed of general dispositions (#3, 11, 14, 27, 28, 37, 55, 60), physical appearance (#1, 24), pedagogical dispositions (#20, 22), and pedagogical competence (#38, 53, 61). The majority of the participants (n = 236, 73.8 per cent) belonged to this cluster. The cluster C3 was featured by four items (#28, hardworking,

#53, clever; #55, caring; #60, kind) Forty-seven (14.7 per cent) of the participants belonged to this cluster. Table 2.1a and Table 2.1b summarise the results discussed above.

TABLE 2.1a   Characteristics of a good teacher

	Items	M	SD	Rank	C1	C2	C3
28	Hardworking	4.49	0.96	1	4	5	5
1	Neat and tidy	4.43	1.06	2	3	5	4
3	Knowledgeable	4.42	1.00	3	3	5	4
11	Helpful	4.41	1.04	4	3	5	4
60	Kind	4.38	1.07	5	3	5	5
61	Able to communicate well with students	4.36	1.06	6	3	5	4
27	Friendly	4.35	1.05	7.5	3	5	4
37	Intelligent	4.35	1.14	7.5	2	5	4
14	Clever/smart	4.33	1.07	10	3	5	4
38	Conducts interesting lessons	4.33	1.12	10	3	5	4
53	Help students to do well in the examination/test	4.33	1.22	10	3	5	5
24	Clean	4.31	1.12	13	3	5	4
22	Sets a good example for students	4.31	1.14	13	3	5	4
20	Has a clear voice (#20)	4.31	1.11	13	3	5	4
55	Caring	4.22	1.23	15	2	5	5
50	Does good quality work	4.18	1.21	16	3	4	4
52	Confident	4.15	1.22	17	3	4	3
30	Patient	4.13	1.16	19	2	4	4
49	Thinks fast	4.13	1.19	19	3	4	4
25	Able to understand similarities and differences	4.13	1.23	19	3	4	3
47	Has many ideas	4.10	1.23	21	2	4	4
29	Conduct group work/project work	4.08	1.23	22.5	3	4	4
26	Has good relation with students, especially those with ideas	4.08	1.13	22.5	3	4	4
41	Recognises good ideas	4.06	1.19	24	3	4	4
62	Think logically and critically	4.03	1.22	25	2	4	4
45	Uses many materials and different ways of teaching	3.99	1.18	26	3	4	4
2	Rewards pupils when they do well	3.96	1.25	27	3	4	4
54	Well-dressed	3.92	1.32	28.5	2	4	3
10	Energetic	3.92	1.33	28.5	3	4	4
23	Optimistic (always thinks positive)	3.90	1.31	30	3	4	3
44	Fair and just	3.88	1.35	31	3	4	4

TABLE 2.1b   Characteristics of a good teacher

	Items	M	SD	Rank	C1	C2	C3
58	Has interest in many areas	3.85	1.27	32	3	4	4
40	Connects ideas with real things, uses real life examples	3.83	1.29	33	2	4	3
5	Good in sports	3.71	1.32	34	3	4	4
46	Able to make/invent things	3.70	1.27	35	2	4	3
7	Makes up rules as he/she goes along	3.68	1.42	36	2	4	3
39	Funny, with sense of humour	3.67	1.42	37	3	4	4
13	Adventurous	3.64	1.35	38	3	4	4
12	Decorates the classroom well	3.60	1.37	39.5	3	4	3
6	Conducts outdoor lesson	3.60	1.39	39.5	3	4	4
35	Conducts quizzes and games in lessons	3.57	1.43	41.5	3	4	4
21	Carefree, full of fun	3.57	1.40	41.5	3	4	4
17	Imaginative	3.55	1.38	43	2	4	3
8	Flexible	3.53	1.42	44	3	4	3
32	Uses visual aids in lessons	3.52	1.44	45	3	4	3
18	Use of computer/video show in lessons	3.45	1.43	46	3	4	3
36	Good in Art and Craft	3.44	1.38	47	3	4	4
4	Firm and strict	3.40	1.36	48	3	4	3
9	Asks difficult questions	3.37	1.36	49	3	4	2
48	Inquisitive	3.29	1.42	50	3	4	2
59	Risk taking	3.27	1.51	51	3	4	3
15	Good in Music	3.25	1.35	52	3	4	3
56	Tries to do what others think is not possible	3.22	1.45	53	3	3	2
42	Unconventional (does not follow old methods)	3.20	1.43	54	3	3	3
57	Keeps trying/experimenting without knowing if he/she is right	3.18	1.48	55	3	3	3
34	Different from others	3.07	1.49	56	3	3	3
16	Pretty/handsome	3.05	1.62	57	3	3	4
51	Prefers to be alone	2.41	1.53	58	3	3	2
43	Day-dreamer	1.88	1.44	59	3	2	2

Table 2.1a and Table 2.1b display final cluster centres of the responses. Discriminant analysis on the responses was performed according to the clusters showed that 92.4 per cent of the participants were correctly classified. The same analysis was done according to gender.

TABLE 2.2   Distribution of the participants according to gender (n, %)

Children's perceptions of a good teacher	Gender	
	Female	Male
C1	12 (7.6)	25 (15.3)
C2	120 (76.4)	116 (71.2)
C3	25 (12.9)	22 (13.5)

The percentage of participants correctly classified was 70.7 per cent. Table 2.2 displays final cluster centres and distributions of the participants.

There was main gender effect ($F1, 304 = 1.39, p < .05$). The male participants rated asking difficult questions significantly higher than did the female participants. The female participants in turn rated twelve items significantly higher than did the male participants: Well-dressed, helpful, conduct outdoor activities, good in music, good in art and craft, friendly, conduct interesting lessons, has a clear voice, conduct group and project work, hard working, caring, and kind. The absolute mean difference between female and male participants were less than 0.5 (between 0.24 and 0.41).

DISCUSSION

Implicit Theories

In general, the children of this study rated a good teacher with a wide range of mean (1.89–4.49). The children did not rate non-conformist qualities highly such as day dreaming, unconventional, different from others, being alone. Diligence, qualities for cognitive competence (e.g., clever, intelligent, knowledgeable, thinking fast, recognising ideas, thinking logically and critically), interpersonal dispositions (e.g., kind, helpful, friendly, caring), general dispositions or image of a person (e.g., clean, neat and tidy, patient, confident) were important qualities for a good teacher. A good teacher should set a good example, help students in examination, and bring out high quality work. He/she has a good voice, and is able to communicate well with the students. Moderately important qualities of a good teacher are related to variations in teaching activities (outdoor, group work, project work), using teaching aids (visual, computer, video), competence in asking questions, and competence in non-examinable subjects (e.g., music, art and craft). Other qualities that were regarded as moderately important include teachers' disciplinary characteristics (e.g., setting rules, firm, strict, fair and just), and innovative qualities (e.g., imaginative, being able to invent, risk-taking, adventurous). From the rank order (mean: 4 and above), children seemed to give a relatively similar degree of importance for qualities of a good teacher and qualities of a creative teacher. Nearly all items of the first thirty ranks in the list of a good teacher were found in the list for a creative teacher. The findings of the paired-t-test for children's ratings on qualities of a good creative and a creative teacher (see Raslinda & Tan, 2003) showed that more items for the last thirty ranks than the first thirty ranks showed significant differences (mean difference less than 0.05). The children seem to consider diligence, cognitive competence, interpersonal dispositions, general dispositions, and pedagogical dispositions (e.g., setting good examples, clear voice and rewarding students) slightly more important for a good teacher than for a creative teacher (see Raslinda & Tan, 2003). In contrast, they seem to regard innovative dispositions, non-conformist dispositions, variations in teaching strategies, and competence in non-examinable subjects (art, music) as slightly more important for a creative teacher than for a good teacher. Based on these observations, we may suggest that in general the Singaporean children are likely to attach 'serious' connotations to a good teacher, and "playful" meanings to a creative teacher.

Specifically, about one tenth of the children considered diligence (working hard) the only quality of a good teacher (C1). Nearly three fourths of them regarded all qualities but the non-conformist and competence in non-examinable subjects (C2). Fifteen per cent of the children regarded most of the qualities for a good teacher except non-conformist and innovative characteristics (C3). While the clusters demonstrated a clear pattern for children's ratings on important qualities of a good teacher, the clusters for qualities of a creative teacher displayed a less distinct pattern. Thirteen percent of the children rated all items moderately or low (C1). Nearly half of them rated all items high (final cluster centre 4 and above) (C3). Slightly more than one third of them rated most items except non-conformist and competence in non-examinable subjects (C2).

Gender Diversity

The female children of the study rated 14 items for a good teacher significantly different from their male counterparts. These items included decorating the classroom well, flexibility, outfit (well-dressed), helpfulness, conducting outdoor activities, competence in music, cleanliness, clear voice, conducting group and project work, working hard, competence in arts and craft, friendliness, being caring, and conducting interesting lessons. The female children rated higher than their male counterparts' items related to pedagogical competence (e.g., conducting outdoor activities and interesting lessons) and interpersonal dispositions (e.g., being caring, helpful and friendly, and having a clear voice). As a matter of fact, in the Singapore's elementary schools, there are more female than male teachers. Future studies should find out if the children's ratings are due to inadequate role-models of male teachers. Or female children's ratings are in general higher than those of male children.

Suggestions for Future Studies

The study assumed that the children under the new educational initiatives in schools have been exposed to various dispositions, pedagogical competence, and learning activities that can foster creativity. From the findings, we may question the practical classroom experiences of the children. Do children in their everyday classroom activities have ample contact with the environment and its resources that can uncover and nurture their potentials? Culture of creativity is developmental. Teachers, as social agents, have to attempt to create local classroom environments that can help the individual children to realise the importance of being creative. Children are capable of constructing the meanings of creative activities and performance through imitation, discovery, and other classroom activities. Teachers' dispositions and competence are composed of the "resources" of the local social structure, the classroom. The individual as a subculture of the classroom should take part actively in various learning activities. It is thus indispensable for future studies to find out if in the actual classrooms, children have enough opportunities to construct meanings for creative activities and performances, and if children's conceptions of creativity match those of the literature. The findings also suggest that more efforts are needed to make creative learning and learning to be creative a part of elementary classroom culture.

Compared to qualities of a good teacher which seem to be more culturally embedded (across ethnicity more significantly different items), the qualities of a creative teacher seem to be less culturally oriented (see Raslinda & Tan, 2003). Two explanations can be given to this observation. First, nation-wide creativity education has not been ingrained into children's everyday life. Home environment and school climate are yet to be stimulating enough for creative performances. Second, complement to the first reason, the concept of "good" is a fundamental human concept that every child first learns through enculturation, acculturation, and socialisation processes. Children may thus have a distinct conception of what constitutes good qualities.

CHAPTER 3

Children's Experiences in the English Language Classroom

DIANAROS AB MAJID AND TAN AI-GIRL

INTRODUCTION

The released of the "Thinking Schools, Learning Nation" (Goh, 1997) framework stimulated a shift in the curriculum. The new textbooks after the year 2001 feature the explicit inclusion of thinking skills. Schools are encouraged to modify their teaching methods, with a shift from a predominantly teacher directed, teacher controlled approach to a teacher-pupil interactive system in which discovery learning is an integral part of the process. The revision of the primary and secondary school syllabus in 2001 includes a change in the focus as well as in the ways the English Language is taught (EL CPDD, 2003). Literacy development is the heart of the English Language instructional program with the teacher as the model of appropriate language use. The guiding principles of language learning and teaching based on the revised 2001 EL syllabus includes the following:

- learner centeredness
- process orientation
- integration
- contextualisation
- spiral progression

Basically language learning and teaching are organised around three major areas of language use namely;

- language for information where the learner will access, retrieve, evaluate, apply and present information derived from print, non-print and electronic resources.

- language for literacy response and expression where the learner will respond creatively and critically to literary texts, relate them to personal experience, culture and society, and use language creatively to express self and identity.

- language for social interaction where the learner will use English effectively both in its spoken and written form to establish and maintain positive interpersonal relationships, taking into account the purpose, audience, context and culture (from EL CPDD, 2003).

In order to successfully achieve the three major areas of language use, it is necessary for language teachers to create a positive learning environment in which pupils feel free to take risks—to stretch themselves in language and in thought (Templeton, 1991). The promotion of creativity in the classroom, however, does not demand teachers to forsake the curriculum and to accept unruly and uncontrollable behaviours; neither does it mean that teachers have to set their sights on achieving scientific, technological, artistic or other revolutionary inventions from all their pupils (Cropley, 1992). With proper planning and a strong belief in the importance of creativity in teaching, it is possible to foster creativity in the classroom.

As research has shown, creativeness does not necessarily only occur by chance or luck (Houtz, 1994). Therefore teachers should consider effective instructional strategies where creativity can be, at the same time infused in the process of learning. This can be achieved if the teacher consciously develops and promotes a strong knowledge base involving activity in a field, builds a rich stock of information, and cultivates appropriate attitudes, values and skills in the pupils (Cropley, 1992). Furthermore, since research has proven that the promotion of creative potentials brings benefits to the individual in terms of better learning and improved mental health (Cropley, 1992) as well as benefits to the society (Walberg & Stariha, 1992), it becomes more necessary that pupils are provided with opportunities to exercise their creative talents.

Most fundamentally though, in order for these creative techniques to be effective it is vital for teachers to believe that there is an urgent need for them to promote creativity in their pupils. To achieve this, teachers need to reflect on their teaching methods and seriously consider modifying their teaching strategies in order to effectively and explicitly include creativity stimulating exercises and consider instructional approach that emphasise skills such as:

- recognising, discovering and inventing,
- seeing connections, similarities and logical implications, and
- making remote associations, accepting primary process materials and forming new gestalts (Cropley, 1997).

Torrance (1972) in his article *Teaching for Creativity* provided the most apt summary of the possibility of teaching creativity especially among children: "It is becoming popular to maintain that that 'nobody can teach anybody anything'. When I teach children and see that creative thinking comes so naturally to most children, I vacillate on this issue myself. Yet, when I find that children who are not being taught are so disabled as creative thinkers, I see how necessary teaching is." (Torrance, 1972: 190) While modifying teaching techniques is important in order to improve pupils' potential in producing creative output, teachers too, need to be effective role models (Amabile, 1996; Zuckerman, 1977) by sharing personal creative work and having greater tolerance towards creative individuals/pupils and their attempts at creative outputs. Rosenthal, Baratz and Hall's (1974) study shows that teachers whose pupils' shows the greatest gains in creativity were rated by classroom observers as being significantly more likeable, more interested in the pupils, more enthusiastic, more professional and more encouraging.

Assumptions and Research Questions

In this chapter, we report on children's views of the English classroom that adopted a creative teaching approach to learning. The framework of creative teaching (Tan, 2000) was referred to when we designed learning activities for the English language lesson. Also referred were the findings of the studies on children's desirable learning activities and their perceived useful learning activities to help them to become creative persons (see Chapter 1). The teacher who was the action researcher (i.e., Dianaros) had about a decade of teaching experience. She carried out and designed an intervention program for creative writing using Internet and a creative technique (SCAMPER) (see Dianaros et al, 2003). In total she has been involved in creativity research for about five years. We assume in this study that creativity is domain specific (see Amabile, 1983). Other assumptions underlying our study are as follows:

- All pupils have the potentials to be creative (see Gardner, 1983).
- Creativity is the resultant process of thinking that has occurred within the individual.
- The end product of creative abilities can be observed and measured.
- Children are creative, although the level of creativeness varies (Beck, 1999).
- Creativity can be increased by deliberate encouragement, opportunity, and training (Beck, 1999).

Accordingly, our research questions are as follows:

- What is the pupils' understanding of the term creativity?
- What types of language learning activities provide pupils with opportunities to exercise their creativity?
- Do creative teaching strategies help pupils to learn the English language better?
- How would pupils want English to be taught in the classroom?

THE STUDY

Participants

A total of 77 primary five pupils (age between 10 to 11 years old) participated in this study. The pupils come from the two English language classes which the researcher is teaching. The pupils have been formally streamed according to their academic performance during the Primary Four Streaming Examination. And all of them have adequate level of language proficiency and ample competence in reading, writing, listening and speaking.

Procedures

The study was conducted from January to October 2003. In all, ten English themes were included in the study. The themes were taken from the compulsory English texts for all pupils currently in Primary Five.

Among the themes selected were "Outer Space Adventure," "Inventors and Inventions," "Travels and Travellers" and "All in the Family." The themes which were selected provide ample opportunities for pupils to discuss and share their personal experiences. The topics covered were also diverse enough to cater to the different interests of the pupils. As such pupils benefited from the exchange of ideas and information.

Basically, the English lessons were planned in line with the goals of the English language objectives for Singapore's primary school pupils:

- Offering a variety of language learning experiences that are both teacher planned and spontaneous.
- Encouraging active participation of pupils as a natural method of learning in such essential areas as speaking, reading, listening and writing.
- Providing sufficient stimuli and opportunities for pupils to express themselves and to use language appropriate for a purpose and situation.
- Encouraging the integration of language skills and thinking skills.

The researcher who is the English teacher of the two classes involved in the study had ample opportunity to be with the pupils in an authentic environment. In all, each class had 12 periods (6 hours) of English lessons per week. Apart from explicit teaching of grammar rules and conventions, the teacher/researcher made use of the English periods to involve pupils in a variety of activities which allow them to harness and display their creativity.

Each of the English lessons was planned such that they seamlessly integrated the four core areas of language learning of reading listening, speaking and writing. Pupils were given sufficient time for interaction while ensuring that the teacher provided a role model of appropriate language use. Table 3.1 shows a sample breakdown of a 2-week lesson plan based on the theme "Travel and Travellers" (Note: each theme has to be covered within a time span of two weeks).

Assessment

Assessment was based on class work done by the pupils. Apart from that pupils were also asked to fill up a self-designed survey form (Creative Teaching and Learning Feedback form, refer to Appendix 3.1) at the end

TABLE 3.1 Breakdown of two week lessons

	Week 1 (structured)	Week 2 (incidental/application)
Monday	Oral interaction- pupils' own experiences of traveling (bring photos for discussion)	Reading fiction based on story books Gulliver Travel, Robinson Crusoe and Vocabulary Expansion
Tuesday	Reading for information based on a given text (refer to PETS)	Creative Group Project—making a brochure (refer to appendix 3.2 for sample of lesson plan)
Wednesday	Vocabulary development	Listening—based on a CD Group presentation—brochure
Thursday	Reading and understanding-based on given comprehension passage	Group writing—based on a given situation (use flipchart) Presentation and peer/class edit
Friday	Language use- adverbials of time and place/location	Individual writing—based on a given situation

of term three just before they sat for their final year examination in the beginning of November. To further validate the study, pupils' performance in mid year and end of year English language examination as well as qualitative assessment which involved informal interviews with pupils and references to pupils' journals were also carried out.

RESULTS AND DISCUSSION

Based on the findings of the survey, pupils seemed to associate the term "creativity" with positive terms. When asked to identify words related to the term "creativity" 64 of them associated the term with the word "interesting." Most of them also associated the term "creativity" with words such as "fun" and "imaginative." Below are the seven top most commonly selected words in the survey forms. Less than 10 per cent of the respondents picked "rigid" and "common" as terms associated with "creativity" while no one selected "boring" as an appropriate term to

TABLE 3.2 Top seven words associated with creativity

	Words associated with creativity	n	%
1	Interesting	64	83.1
2	Fun	58	75.3
3	Imaginative	57	74.0
4	Challenging	50	64.9
5	Unique	46	59.7
6	New	33	42.8
7	Different	30	38.9

describe "creativity". Based on this information, it reaffirmed the assumption that pupils were aware of what constitute a creative lesson and were able to cite useful examples of creative inducing activities that had and could be done in the classrooms. Table 3.2 displays the pupils' responses of the top seven words associated with creativity.

Subsequently, pupils were asked to recall activities which they had done in class that had an impact in improving their creativity. Fifty-seven pupils identified project work and group work as activities that provided them with the highest opportunity to exercise their creativity (see Appendix 3.3). This was followed by games and brainstorming sessions. Pupils also seemed to feel that composition exercises helped them improve their creativity. When pupils were interviewed further and questioned on why they had chosen composition writing as a creative inducing activity, more that 45 per cent of them pointed out that the variety of pre writing activities used had assisted them in writing more creative compositions. Pupils also cited interesting and relevant composition topics given had also helped to heighten their interest and at the same time stimulate their creativity. Table 3.3 shows a list of activities which the pupils have identified as being effective in promoting their creativity while at the same time providing them with ample opportunities to learn the English Language.

Pupils were then asked to list down activities which they wished to have more of during their English lessons. Based on the responses, pupils preferred activities which involved active participation and at the same time give them a chance to exercise their aural and oral skills. When pupils were interviewed to find out more about their choices, they shared

TABLE 3.3 Top five activities that enhance creativity

	Activities that help enhance creativity	n	%
1	Project work/group work	57	74.0
2	Language/ word games	55	71.4
3	Brainstorming	53	68.8
4	Composition writing	52	67.5
5	Internet searching	49	63.6

that learning English became more interesting and meaningful when they had a chance to practise what they were learning in "play-like" and "non-threatening" situations such as in role play, drama and games. Pupils also pointed out that internet searching was much preferred as it provided them with interesting visual stimulus as well as the ability to find out necessary information and facts in greater depth and at differing pace. The responses also seemed to suggest that pupils preferred interacting and doing work in groups or as a class to working in solitude. Table 3.4 shows a list of activities that pupils would want to have more of in their English lessons.

When pupils were asked if they enjoyed their English lessons so far, 48 of them (62.3 per cent) responded "yes definitely," 26 (33.8 per cent) responded "mostly" with one (1.3 per cent) responding "slightly." Subsequently when they were asked if the English lessons included a variety of creative activities, 14 (18.2 per cent) of them responded "all the time," 52 (67.5 per cent) of them responded "most of the time" while 10 (7.7 per cent) responded "sometimes." Finally when the pupils were asked to recall if the creative activities help them to learn English better,

TABLE 3.4 Top five activities pupils liked to have more

	Activities that pupils would like to have	n	%
1	Language/word games	53	68.8
2	Internet searching	45	58.4
3	Project work/group work	38	49.3
4	Debate	30	38.9
5	Role play	28	36.4

34 (44.2 per cent) of them stated "yes definitely," 38 (49.4 per cent) of them responded "mostly" while 5 (6.5 per cent) of them responded "slightly."

Apart from the survey, pupils were also interviewed randomly and were asked the questions:

- Do you think that the English lessons have been taught differently from the way you were taught in the previous years? How?
- Do you think it has helped in improving your performance in English? Explain.

All the pupils who were interviewed (ten in all participated voluntarily) agreed that the English lessons have been taught in a very interesting manner. They used words/phrases such as "fun yet educational," "interesting," "not boring" and "look forward" to describe the English lessons. The pupils interviewed also commended the teacher for being "supportive and enthusiastic in her teaching" and that "she has made the learning of English more meaningful and yet exciting." Pupils interviewed were able to give examples of "creative" activities which they have done in class and which they felt have helped them in learning the language. Among the examples cited were "making posters, newsletters and pamphlets," "surfing the Internet for information," "playing language games," "debates" and "quiz and role plays."

The pupils interviewed felt that the "creative" language learning activities which were employed have not in any way hampered them in their language learning. In fact they felt that the activities have spurred them to learn the language in greater depth and have in fact helped them improved their vocabulary as well as their aural and oral skills tremendously.

To further validate the study, reference was made to pupils' performance for their mid and final year English examinations. Table 3.5 gives a summary of pupils' performance for both the mid-year as well as the final year examinations. Based on the results, except for one pupil who had opted to be in the EM2 stream (taking the English language as the first language and mother tongue as the second language) instead of the allotted EM3 (taking the English language and the mother tongue as the second language), all other pupils have showed improvement in their English performance with more pupils getting quality passes.

TABLE 3.5 Pupils' performance in the English language

	Mid-year exam		Final year exam	
	n	%	n	%
Band 1: 85-100 marks	6	7.8	10	13.0
Band 2: 70-84 marks	55	71.4	56	72.2
Band 3: 50-69 marks	18	23.4	13	18.8
Band 4: below 50 marks	1	1.3	1	1.3

Upon reflection, pupils' were generally enthusiastic and participated actively during class activities and presentation. Pupils enjoyed the less structured group activities which allow them the freedom to come up with creative outputs such as their own version of newspapers and travel brochures. At the same time they welcomed the more structured lessons which involved serious explanation of grammar rules and other necessary rudiments of language learning as well as "revision worksheets." Pupils were very cordial with one another and with the researcher and were able to relate to one another effectively. In all, pupils appreciated the combination of structured and incidental method of language learning and welcomed the less than "traditional method" of learning English which included a balance of "creative activities" and "drill and practice" exercises.

CONCLUDING REMARKS

In an attempt to promote creativity in the English language classroom, it is important to consider the process of language teaching and learning. It is vital to include the role that teachers need to play in the process of fostering creative thinking in the pupils under their charge. It has become increasingly apparent that children only display creativity when they want to and when they feel able to (Cropley, 1997). In the classroom environment, the teacher is therefore the most fundamental person who is able to make or break the creative potentials of her pupils. A teacher can directly reinforce creativity through her interaction with the pupils by rewarding their creative efforts (process) and outcomes (product) as well as recognising their creative traits (person). The teacher can also indirectly influence pupils' creativity by creating a supportive social environment through her words and deeds (Soh, 2000). A supportive learning environment is essential for nurturing creative behaviour and personalities.

In addition pupils need appropriate skills and abilities, such as the capacity to recognise inconsistencies and to get ideas. Bloom (1985) in his studies of the factors that led to the emergence of creative potential in young people showed that in many cases a single significant person played a crucial role for making the person aware of his potential. This can be done by a teacher who demonstrated passionate interest in a topic and awakened it in the child (Cropley, 1997). Furthermore, teachers who adopt unconventional roles and approaches can be more effective in enhancing pupils' creative abilities than teachers who follow traditional instructional approaches (Esquivel, 1995).

Combining summaries such as those of Cropley (1992), Soh (2000) and Torrance (1992) suggest that teachers should value and promote in their pupils properties such as:

- task commitment, persistence and determination
- curiosity, adventurousness and tolerance for ambiguity.
- independence and non-conformity
- self confidence and willingness to risk being wronged
- drive to experiment and willingness to try difficult task.

However it is not sufficient for teachers to only provide creative inducing environment in the class. The teachers themselves need to work on becoming more creative. Cropley (1982) pointed out that "creative inducing" teachers provide a model of creative behaviour, reinforce such behaviour when students display it and establish a classroom atmosphere that is supportive of creativity. Listed below are six skills suggested by Downing (1977) for creative teaching:

- Managing—establishing an orderly work environment that honours inquiry and creative expression.
- Presenting—presenting material in a lively, organised manner that calls for frequent responses from students.
- Questioning—asking questions that stimulate students to think about connections, alternatives and new possibilities.

- Designing—designing a wide variety of activities that allow the whole class to be fully engaged in constructive learning all the time.
- Running activities—providing activities that lead students to develop creative initiatives as well as mastery of skills.
- Relating—communicating caring and concern for student's progress in original thinking and creative expression.

In the classroom, teachers and children are two interdependent systems. As partners, teachers and children work together to construct effective and stimulating learning environment indispensable to assist children to unfold their creative potentials. In "education for being" creativity should be taken as the outcomes of personal growth. Accordingly, children should be given the opportunities for creative expression (Jalongo, 2003). Children should be offered the right to express their own feeling, to reflect upon their own behaviour, to ask questions, to seek explanations in natural world, to love and be loved, to name just a few. They should be allowed to experience internal freedoms (e.g., thought, desires, purposes, observations and judgment) and external freedom (e.g., speech and movement) (see e.g., Dewey, 1937/2002). The findings of our study, in line with this standpoint, suggest rewarding engagement of children in learning.

Note: *Dianaros Majid is the first author of this chapter.

APPENDIX 3.1

Creative Teaching and Learning Form
(Feedback for the English Language Lessons)

Age: _____

1) Do you enjoy your English lessons?

Yes, definitely ☐ mostly ☐ slightly ☐ No, definitely ☐

2a) State the reason why you enjoyed the English language lessons:

2b) If you did not enjoy the lessons, then state the reasons:

3) Circle the words which you feel are associated with the term creativity.

original	new	interesting	confusing
strange but relevant	common	different from the usual	
challenging	fun	imaginative	routine
novel	not common	surprising	boring
useful	refreshing	unique	rigid

4) Do your English lessons include a variety of 'creative' activities?

All the time ☐ most of the time ☐ sometimes ☐ never ☐

5) Give 3 examples of 'creative' activities that you have done during your EL lessons.

a)

b)

c)

6) Do you think the 'creative' activities help you to learn English better?

Yes, definitely ☐ mostly ☐ slightly ☐ No, definitely ☐

7) Do you think the teacher has made an effort to make the lessons more 'creative' and enjoyable?

All the time ☐ most of the time ☐ sometimes ☐ never ☐

8) Do you think the teacher appreciates your creative ideas during activities such as group work, composition writing, class activities and discussions?

All the time ☐ most of the time ☐ sometimes ☐ never ☐

9) Does the teacher criticise your idea/work if it is not up to her expectations?

All the time ☐ most of the time ☐ sometimes ☐ never ☐

10a) Read the list of activities below and add a (√) to those which you think give you a chance to exercise your creativity.

	statements	√	*		statements	√	*
1	role play			6	worksheets		
2	brainstorming			7	project work/group work		
3	SCAMPER			8	show and tell		
4	internet searching			9	composition		
5	debate			10	games		

10b) Now read the list (above) again and add a (*) to those activities that you would like to have more of during your English language lessons.

11) If you have a chance to come up with a creative and enjoyable English language lesson, how would it be? You may share your ideas below.

Thank You for Your Participation!

APPENDIX 3.2 A sample lesson plan based on the theme "travels and travellers"

Skill focus	Area of language use/text type	Suggested activities	Resources	Time frame
Reading and Writing (extension to grammar and vocabulary lessons)	Language for Information (information text-brochures/ itinerary)	Pupils to bring at least three different brochures/itineraries related to Singapore and various tourist attractions.	Brochures/ itineraries	Three periods
		Teacher to show some examples from the Singapore Tourism Board e.g., Sentosa, Singapore Zoo, and Bird Park.	Construction papers	
		Pupils to work in their groups to skim through the different brochures to find out the similar information that are found. Suggest to pupils to look for text markers like **subheadings** to get a brief overview of what is written.		
		Pupils to list similar information on the board e.g., places of interest, accommodation, transport, currency, and weather. Discuss why is each one important in a brochure.		
		Pupils to look at the ways, in which the information in the different brochures is presented. Guiding questions: – What is important when deciding how to structure information in this text type? – What information needs to be included in a brochure to provide information for first time tourist coming to Singapore? Point out the use of the following structures: Imperatives – enjoy the wonderful, spend a day or two Adjectives – leisurely Present tense		
		Pupils to come up with a brochure on behalf of the Singapore Tourism Board to attract tourists to Singapore		

APPENDIX 3.3 A sample lesson plan based on the theme "curtain call"

Skill focus	Area of language use/text type	Suggested activities	Resources	Time frame
Oral Interaction / discussion (extension to grammar/ vocabulary lessons)	Language for literary response / expression (narrative texts)	Week 1: Pupils to view parts of the movie 'Wizard of Oz'. Pupils to take down notes on • how the main character was transported to Oz land • the special attributes of each character in the story • their wishes and what they got Discuss the play with the class after viewing it. Pupils to share new terms and interesting phrases that they have noted down while watching the movie.	VCD of Wizard of Oz	Two periods (week 2, one hour)
		Pupils to refer to the textbook for an excerpt of the play. Pupils work in groups. They are given one week to rehearse their parts to be acted out in front of the class on the following week. Some pupils scrap materials for props and simple costumes. Note: Pupils to take note of the layout of the text, and of the importance of expression in reading. ** Encourage pupils to work on their play when they have completed their daily classroom work.	Some scrap materials for simple props and costumes	Two periods (week 2, one hour)
		Week 2 Groups to present their play. Invite other pupils to give comments and share what they like about the presentation and what need to be improved. Point out the importance of props, facial expression as well as voice projection and intonation in the presentation.	A scene from the play Wizard of Oz – dialogue for role play (refer to textbook)	Total: Four periods (two hours)
		Pupils to write one page reflection on what they learned in the process of coming up with their own play.	Flipchart papers	

CHAPTER 4

Secondary School Students' Perceptions of Choral Learning

TAN AI-GIRL AND FLORA YEE

INTRODUCTION

Singapore's Education and Holistic Development

Since 1997, Singapore's educational system has introduced gradually new initiatives aimed to develop every child holistically. The aspiration to educate every child holistically was spelt out implicitly through three national initiatives, and became more explicit in a learning outcome document and its subsequent call for developing every child's potential. The three initiatives were released between April and June, 1997.

The Thinking Schools and a Learning Nation (TSLN, Goh, 1997) framework was read by the Prime Minister at the 7th International Conference on Thinking, with the intent to call for a nationwide involvement in developing a culture of learning beyond high academic achievement (June, 1997). Among the highlights was the need to foster creativity, critical thinking, and problem solving competence. The National Education (NE) program (Lee, 1997) focused on implanting the sense of belongingness among the young. The Information Technology (IT) Master plan (Teo, 1997) implemented programs to upgrade the IT facilities of educational institutions as well as the IT competence of teachers and students.

The essence of these three initiatives was then integrated into a document, the Desired Outcomes of Education (DOE) (MOE, 1998). The DOE spelt out ideal educational outcomes in terms of competencies of students at various school levels and in cognitive (TSLN and IT Master plan) and affective (NE) domains. Subsequent discussions at the policy level focused on compulsory, preschool, early childhood, and special education. The inception of the Ability-Driven Education (ADE) paradigm (MOE, 1999) attempted to integrate the above-mentioned initiatives, educational outcomes, and discussion.

The ADE delineated more explicitly the importance of individual differences, the uniqueness of every child, and opportunities for all. Along this ADE paradigm, the School Excellence Model (SEM, 2003) was introduced to empower school leaders to identify their staff's strengths and niche areas for improvement. Underlying this model was the awareness of promoting staff welfare and students' wellness. The move to holistic education has been piecemeal and gradual. At times, it has appeared challenging, as the philosophy of holistic education might not flow smoothly into a culture of education rooted in a competitive system that implements streaming and ranking.

Co-curricular Activities and Choral Learning

In a holistic educational framework, Singapore's educational system aspires that every student should be given the opportunity to develop optimistically and fully in intellectual, emotional, and interpersonal domains (MOE, 1998). To achieve this, intermediate outcomes of education are delineated. Among them is the cultivation of appreciation of aesthetics through not only the formal classroom curriculum but also the co-curricular activities (CCAs) that each individual school organises. The CCAs serve as healthy recreation. Students learn, through participation in CCAs, some forms of self-discipline and teamwork. The ultimate aim of CCAs is to develop the student's physique and character.

Our chapter examines secondary school students' perceptions of choral learning. We identified choir as our domain of study, as it has been a highly regarded non-academic activity. In line with the nation's aspiration to nurture every person's creative competence in multiple disciplines, choir or music has received substantial support. Choral programs in the secondary schools are developed with the support of the Music Department of the CCA branch at the ministerial level. The support ranges from providing professional instructors attached to schools and organising complimentary workshops for potential choir teachers, to exposing students to large-scale national events, such as the Singapore Youth Festival (SYF) Central Judging, and the National Day Parade.

After six years of elementary education, Singaporean students, based on their Primary School Leaving Examination (PSLE), are streamed to Express, Normal Academic, and Normal Technical streams. They then take the Ordinary level of examination after four years (Express and Normal Technical) or five years (Normal Academic) of secondary schooling. Singapore secondary schools introduce choices in the subject areas and CCAs. For university admission, in 2003, CCAs were given a considering status in addition to the nationwide examination results.

Under the ADE paradigm, students are expected to be active in academic and non-academic disciplines. The introduction of CCAs, for instance, was meant to relate student learning to multidisciplinary exposure and alternative assessment. Specifically, the CCAs can help implant students' awareness to be responsible, healthy, socially engaging, and culturally sensitive citizens. Students learn to take part actively by making choices. They are exposed to authentic experiences that will likely help uncover and develop their potentials in non-academic domains.

Other Rationales of Our Study

Our study examined students' perceptions of choral learning from their personal and interpersonal perspectives, as well as from their interactions with the subject (e.g., contents and structure), their physical environments, and school expectations. A person's perception of the learning environment is constructed with reference to his/her contact and experience with multiple factors. The factors include alternative curricula (Welch & Walberg, 1972), alternative school (Fraser et al, 1987), student and teacher perceptions of the same classroom environment (Fraser, 1984; Raviv et al, 1990), the class (Anderson & Walberg, 1972), and type of school (e.g., spiritual or government, Dorman et al, 1994), just to name a few. Gender, a social category, to some extent can influence a person's view of the learning environment. Studies revealed gender differences in learning environment perceptions. It was found that male pupils preferred a competitive learning environment, in contrast to female pupils' preference for personal and cooperative learning environments (Byrne et al, 1986; Owen & Straton, 1980). Females also held more favourable perceptions of their classroom environments than males (Henderson, Fisher & Fraser, 1995; Fraser et al, 1995; Fisher et al, 1997).

A school class is regarded as a social system (Getzel & Thelen, 1972). The classroom-learning environment is made up of psychosocial factors such as student cohesiveness, self-esteem, confidence, sense of belonging, and motivation (Goh, 2002). A student's learning process is affected by the interpersonal relationship he/she has with his/her teacher (Brekelmans et al, 2002). The learning environment and learning performance are affected by the interrelationships and communications among all members in the classroom community (Doyle, 1979; Goh & Fraser, 2000). Hence, it is indispensable to ensure a positive classroom climate for effective learning.

Recently, in Singapore, most of the studies on learning environments employed adopted questionnaires (Fraser, 2002) or were conducted in laboratory environments (Goh, 2002; Wong et al, 1997). Researchers in the field of learning environments, in the past several decades have selected methods to uncover psychosocial aspects of the classroom-learning environment: direct observation, the assessment of student and teacher perceptions, and case studies (Walberg & Anderson, 1968). Questionnaires have been designed to assess student perceptions of specific teacher behaviours (see e.g., Woods & Fraser, 1995). Survey papers (see e.g., Fisher & Waldrip, 1997) have been developed to assess culturally sensitive learning environmental factors.

Our study on choral learning was exploratory in nature. Instead of using adopted questionnaires, we employed open-ended questions to uncover secondary school students' views of choral learning. Based on their responses and researchers' observations, we designed a questionnaire to examine the following research questions: (1) What are Singapore's secondary school students' perceptions of choral learning? (2) Are there any gender differences in their perceptions of choral learning? (3) Are there any across school differences in their perceptions of choral learning?

METHOD

Participants

In total, 122 secondary school students participated in a paper-and-pencil survey. They were students from two public schools located in the suburbs. There were 83 (68.1 per cent) female and 39 (31.9 per cent) male students. The participants attended weekly choral lessons under the school's non-sport co-curricular activity. Their mean age was 13.6 years old with a standard deviation of .nine years. Nearly half of them (n = 62) were from a school that had an established choral program (more than five years), whereas the other half (n = 60) were from a school with a new choral program (less than five years).

Survey

The survey was developed with main reference to the outcomes of a pilot study participated by 80 secondary school students (age range: 12–17 years old), who attended regular choir lessons to obtain their responses on what they liked and disliked about choir. The students were requested to write one event or aspect each, of what they liked and disliked about choir. In approximately 10 to 15 minutes the students wrote their responses on a piece of paper. The responses were categorised according to themes: "myself" (e.g., I love to sing, and I like to express my feelings), "my instructor" (e.g., she teaches well, and she is caring), "my peers" (e.g., they are friendly, and they are confident), "the choir learning process" (e.g., it is fun), and "choir learning outcomes" (e.g., choir provides us the opportunity to perform). In addition to the outcomes of the pilot study, the researcher communicated with the choir instructor, and added some other relevant items and categories such as the contents of the choir lessons, its structure, and the school's expectations.

The questionnaire for the main study had two sections. Section 1 included items related to demographic information: age, gender, and school and self-report questions related to interest in the choir, and benefits of participating in the choir. Section 2 comprised items describing experiences of choral learning in the following aspects: my-self, my instructor, my choir peers, my school, and the choir contents/structure (see Yee, 2003, for the complete list). The participants were invited to write other comments related to how to improve the choir sessions, and how the choir instructor can motivate them to participate.

Procedure

The questionnaire was distributed to the participants during one of the choral meetings between September and October 2002. The participants first filled in demographic information, and indicated their interest in the choir (yes or no). They then rated the degree of agreeableness of items that described their choral learning on a 5-point scale with anchors of 1: strongly disagree, 2: disagree, 3: agree somewhat, 4: agree, and 5: strongly agree. The following instructions were shown: "*You are invited to fill out a survey that intends to find out your view of choral learning. Your response is voluntary and confidential. There is no right or wrong answer. Please rate the items using a 5-point scale. The rating you choose should correspond closely to your view. Thank you for your participation.*" A sample item was employed to demonstrate how the participants should circle their responses. On average, the participants spent about 10 to 15 minutes to complete the questionnaire.

Results

The descriptive statistics of mean and standard deviation were computed for all items. The skewness and kurtosis of the items were examined. As none of the items had a value of skewness or kurtosis of 1.64 and above (Bauer, 1984), the data were subjected to factor analyses and t-tests. The estimate of Cronbach's alpha for the items related to choral learning (part two) was high, at 0.97. When alpha reaches 0.70 and above, we assume that internal consistency of the instrument exists (Cortine, 1993).

Items with a mean value of 3.5 and above were subjected to further analysis. In total, 31 items were factor analysed and accounted for 65.1 per cent of variance. The Kaiser-Meyer-Olkin Measure of Sampling Adequacy (KMO-MSA, 0.84) and the Approximate Chi-squares (2191.775, df. = 465) from Bartlett's test of sphericity (BTS) were calculated at p less than 0.0001 significant level for each of the scales. The rotation method used was the Oblimin with Kaiser normalisation, and the extraction method was the principal component analysis. Items with a factor loading of 0.30 and above were selected for interpretation. Cronbach's alphas for the six factors were 0.79 and above. Table 4.1 outlines the results of factor analysis and alphas. The co-relations among factors were between −0.30 and 0.40, mainly around 0.20 and 0.30.

The items of each factor were summed, and the sum was divided by the number of items to yield new scores, where mean, standard deviation, final cluster centres and discriminant matrix were computed (see Table 4.2). Cluster analysis sorted the participants into two groups or clusters. Thirty-seven (30.3 per cent) participants belonged to cluster C1, with a final cluster centre for all categories, less than 3.5 except the category "my instructor as classroom manager." Eighty-five (69.7 per cent) participants were grouped to cluster C2, with a final cluster centre for all categories, more than 3.7. The distance between C1 and C2 was 2.2. Discriminant analysis on the two clusters yielded a high percentage (93.4 per cent) of original grouped case being correctly classified.

TABLE 4.1   Secondary students' views of choral learning: Factor analysis and Cronbach's alpha

	Factor loading	Variance	Eigen-Value	Alpha
Myself		30.9	9.6	0.89
I love to sing	0.85			
I like to express my feelings through singing	0.81			
I like to learn more songs	0.71			
I would encourage more students to join the choir	0.64			
I would choose to remain in the choir, even if I have a chance to change to another co-curricular activity	0.64			
For me, the choir is fun	0.61			
My instructor as classroom manager		11.5	3.6	0.86
Selects suitable materials and resources	0.88			
Has a clear voice	0.84			
Is a role model	0.77			
Monitors our progress closely	0.68			
Sets appropriate expectations	0.59			
Rewards our performance appropriately	0.50			
My choral peer		8.5	2.7	0.87
Are friendly, share resources willingly	0.84			
Approachable/easy to make friends with	0.77			
Are united/like each other	0.74			
Are co-operative/work together closely	0.70			
Are confident/have high self-esteem in choir	0.66			
Are motivated/enjoy singing together	0.65			
My school		5.6	1.7	0.81
Encourages the choir to take part in competitions and concerts	−0.80			
Involves the choir sufficiently in school events	−0.80			
Is proud of the choir	−0.75			
Sets appropriate expectations of the choir	−0.66			
The choir contents/structure		5.0	1.5	0.86
The songs are challenging	0.76			
The session is just nice (not too long)	0.75			
There is sufficient number of scores for everyone	0.75			

TABLE 4.1   (cont'd)

The pace of learning is just right	0.73		
The songs are well selected	0.69		
The schedule of the choir is appropriate (I can cope with it)	0.69		
My instructor as facilitator		3.8	1.2	0.79
Expects us to work in a group co-operatively	0.76		
Gives us opportunities to share our strengths and weaknesses	0.74		
Is caring/allows trials and errors and accepts our mistakes	0.55		

TABLE 4.2   Mean, standard deviation, cluster centres and discriminant structure matrix

	M	SD	Final cluster centre, C1	Final cluster centre, C2	Discriminant structure matrix
My instructor as classroom manager	4.11	0.59	3.70	4.28	0.43
My instructor as facilitator	3.90	0.68	3.41	4.11	0.45
My school	3.77	0.77	3.24	4.00	0.50
Myself	3.77	0.89	2.93	4.14	0.67
The choir contents/structure	3.60	0.79	2.88	3.92	0.63
My choral peers	3.46	0.75	2.87	3.71	0.50

NOTE: Functions at group centroids, C1 = –1.81, C2 = 0.79.

The two sample independent t-test was computed for the six factors using the new scores. The t-test yielded significantly different results for female (M = 3.90, SD = 0.80) and male (M = 3.51, SD = 1.01) participants for the category of "myself" (t = –2.28) at $p < 0.05$ level. The same t-test was computed to find out differences between the participants from a school with an established choral program (school 1) and a school with a new choral program (school 2). Participants of school 1 scored significantly higher than their counterparts of school 2 for three categories at the 0.005 and 0.05 levels. (1) Myself (school 1: M = 4.03, SD = 0.62; school 2: M = 3.51, SD = 1.04; t = 3.40), (2) choral curriculum (school 1: M = 3.77, SD = 0.67; school 2: M = 3.43, SD = 0.87; t = 2.47), and my choral peers (school 1: M = 3.63, SD = 0.67; school 2: M = 3.28, SD = 0.80; t = 2.58).

A 2×2 (gender, school) multivariate analysis of variance yielded main school effects ($F_{121, 1}$ = 3.41, p < 0.005). Tests of between-subjects for category of choral contents yielded main effects for school ($F_{121, 1}$ = 11.62, p < 0.005) and school versus gender ($F_{121, 1}$ = 5.15, p < 0.05). The same tests also yielded between subject effects for the categories of myself ($F_{121, 1}$ = 11.35, p < 0.005) and choral peers ($F_{121, 1}$ = 5.14, p < 0.05).

Other comments related to how to improve the choir sessions: In total the participants elicited 91 statements, of which 39 statements were from the participants in school 1 and 52 from those in school 2. The statements were categorised into the instructor, curriculum (schedule, content or activities), choir members and others. Statements from participants in school 2 included views with regard to choir members particularly their concern about leadership and discipline (see Table 4.3).

TABLE 4.3   Feedback on improving choir (examples)

Comments on how to improve the choir:
School 1
The Instructor
078: The instructor should let us choose a song that we would like to sing for warming up.
079: The instructor may want to use construct a song game.

Curriculum: Schedule
099: The choir session must end up early on weekdays.
070: Change CCA schedule to 1 hour on weekday and Saturday.
077: Longer break.

Curriculum: Contents
102: The choir needs more activities, e.g., sing for the community.
087: Have board games before the session.
097: Consider songs that members chose.
109: Have more variety of songs.

Choir Members: Discipline
117: Reduce the noise level of the choir room.
118: Disciplined the members.
066: Choose better leader.

TABLE 4.3   (cont'd)

Others
090: Should have bought more chairs so that we can sit comfortably.
099: Change the choir t-shirt to black.

School 2
Physical Environment
002: Have a better music room.

Teacher/instructor
012: Better teacher.
050: Be more lenient with us.
051: Focus on meeting people needs.

Curriculum: Activities
002: Have more game session.
014: More choir outing like singing with other school during holiday.
035: More new, fresh, interesting way of singing.
025: The session should have more jokes more laughter

Curriculum: Schedule
015: Start earlier.
016: Have sessions more frequently.
017: Shorten the duration.
018: Make the section longer.

Choir Members: Arrangement
002: Position of member can be further improved.

Choir Members: Leadership
037: Get all of them to listen to what the committee says. Respect them.
041: Vice-chairman must not be too 'bossy'.

Choir Members: Discipline
044: Everyone must be puncture. Learn well. Don't play with hand-phone.
031: Talk less during practice.

Suggestions on how the instructor can motivate the participants: In total the participants elicited 66 statements of which 32 were from the participants in school 1 and 34 from those in school 2. The statements were categorised into encouragement, contents, pedagogy, and teacher dispositions. The participants in school 2 raised concern about the instructors' dispositions, but their counterparts in school 1 did not show concern in this area (see Table 4.4).

DISCUSSION

Perceived Choral Learning

The secondary school students rated moderately high choral learning, the perspectives of their instructor (as classroom manager and facilitator), their interest in singing and the choir, their school support for the choir, their peer involvement in the choir, and the contents or structure of the choir (see Table 4.1). This finding is in line with the research framework of the classroom environment, that learning is influenced by psychosocial factors such as self-engagement as well as teacher, peer, and school involvement (see e.g., Fisher & Waldrip, 2002). From means, the Singaporean secondary school students in our study acknowledged highly the instructor's role as classroom manager, and the instructor's role as facilitator. The participants' responses confirmed findings of previous studies on Singaporeans' perceived teacher roles as facilitator in secondary schools and as classroom manager across school levels (Tan, 1999). They agreed moderately with their school's support for choral sessions, their interest in the choir, and the choral structure and contents. They were critical in their peers' social competence and confidence, and rated the related items moderately low (see Table 4.2). Their ratings for physical environments and other teacher roles (e.g., teacher as creator or innovator) were low (M below 3.5; see Yee, 2003). Future studies should revisit the connotations of their low ratings on physical environments and other teacher roles. Do the low ratings indicate less significant or less important, or do they imply the absence of quality?

About one third of the participants (n = 37, 30.33 per cent) belonged to the cluster (C1), where final cluster centre values for nearly all categories were moderately low (between 3.41 and 2.87). Of the total participants in this group, nearly three quarters (n = 26, 70.3 per cent) were from the school with a newly formed choir and choral program

TABLE 4.4   Feedback on ways to motivate (examples)

Suggest to your instructor how she can motivate you to participate:
School 1
Encouragement/Fun
077: Give us sweets or 'titbits' after practice.
080: Give us some words of encouragement.
109: More allowances for mistake.
118: Reward and encouragement. Impart confidence.

Contents
074: Choose better song.
083: More inspiration songs.
092: More outdoor activities.

Pedagogy
067: Sing with us.
082: Get role models from student leaders. Encourage pupils to teach pupils.
079: The instructor may want to let us choose some songs we like.
084: Let us know that the program is good for us. We can learn something from it. Share with us more about music.
086: Be strict and more concern. Do not set too high expectation.
104:   Better communication.

School 2
Content
002: More interesting songs.
049: Have new and more ways to teach us.
002: Organise more exchange programme and concert.

Teacher Disposition
003: Be more friendly.
031: Be more patient with us.
036: Smile more often.
046: Joke with us now and then when teaching.

Encouragement/Award
006: Encourage more and help us to improve our singing.
002: Reward good work.
022: Make choir more enjoyable then now.

Others
002: Dress up nicely, brighter colour.
052: Stricter.

(school 2). More than two thirds of the participants belonged to the cluster (C2), where final cluster centre values for all categories ranged between moderately high (3.71) to high (4.28). Of the total participants in this group, sixty per cent (n = 51) were from the school with an established choir program and a long history of choral culture (school 1). The composition of members according to gender was similar for the two clusters, resembling the percentage of female and male participants of the study. This finding seems to suggest that school choral culture to a certain extent influences the participants' views on choral learning in relation to the instructor's behaviour to their motivation or interest, the school's support, their peers' social and personal competence, and the choir's structure and contents. We shall discuss this observation further in the forthcoming session under the sub-heading 'School Difference'.

Gender Difference

Female participants in the study rated nearly all categories higher than their male counterparts. The former group rated the category "myself" significantly higher than the latter. Our results supported findings of the earlier research, that females held more favourable perceptions than males, of classroom environments (Henderson et al, 1995; Fraser et al, 1995; Fisher et al, 1997). Research has shown that a competitive learning environment was the preference of male students, whereas female students' preferred a personal and cooperative learning environment (Byrne et al, 1986; Owen & Straton, 1980). Future studies should attempt to capture the culture of a competitive learning environment.

School Difference

From means, the participants in our study differed in their perceptions of choral learning significantly in three aspects: myself, school, and choral curriculum; those in School 1 rated higher than those in School 2. To find out differences in the participants' perceptions across schools, we referred to the self-report responses with regards to voluntary or assigned participation. Two-thirds to three-quarters of the participants in School 1 joined the choir voluntarily (n = 41, 66.1 per cent) and were encouraged by others (n = 45, 72.6 per cent). One-third of them were assigned to join the choir (n = 120, 32.3 per cent). In contrast, less than half of the participants from School 2 voluntarily participated in the choir (n = 29,

48.3 per cent) and were encouraged by others (n = 26, 43.3 per cent). Instead, sixty per cent (n = 36) of them were assigned to the choir, i.e., they were not given a choice.

We attribute the differences in perceptions of choral learning in the areas of personal interest (myself) and the quality of choir members' participation (how committed the choral peers were in learning together) to the presence of choice in school 1 and absence of choice in school 2. Our field observations noted the following remarks. In School 1, recruitment of choir members was based on students' personal interest and through the encouragement of teachers or peers. Joining the School 1 choir was on a voluntary basis. However, in School 2, all first year secondary school students were subjected to an audition or a selection test for some CCAs, including the choir. Once the student has passed the audition, he/she would be allocated a place, regardless of his/her interest in the choir. The student could appeal to opt out, but only a handful of them succeeded.

The two schools engaged the same instructor. Hence, there was no difference in the students' ratings of their perceptions in this area.

The participants from School 1 had a significantly higher rating than their counterparts in School 2 for choir contents and structure. In School 1, the choir was allowed to have the choice of pieces (including spiritual songs), and to pace the rate of learning. In contrast, school 2 had a structured schedule of learning and limited the selection of songs. The results of our study show that school culture to a certain extent influences students' perceptions of learning.

Holistic Education

There was nearly no difference in percentage for statements related to "choir creates opportunities to make friends" (school 1: n = 58, 93.5 per cent; school 2: n = 56, 93.3 per cent), and 'choir nurtures creativity' (school 1: n = 43, 69.4 per cent; school 2: n = 41, 68.3 per cent). Nearly all participants regarded the choir as a social activity to get to know new friends, and two-thirds of them considered choral education as part of creative education. To establish a positive and creative choral learning environment, we refer to Wills' (1995) recommendations for dance, for some insights. Taking the Singaporean choral learning environment into perspective, it is indispensable to establish a non-threatening and professional relationship and communication between the instructor, the school, and the choir members. The three parties must come to terms to set common goals to optimise the choir members' learning outcomes.

From the self-reported responses, the majority of the participants in School 1 agreed to the statements that "choir makes their day pretty" (n = 54, 87.1 per cent), "choir removes stress" (n = 50, 80.6 per cent), and "choir enhances intelligence" (n = 54, 87.1 per cent). A lesser percentage of the participants in School 2 agreed to these statements: "choir makes my day pretty" (n = 36, 60 per cent), "choir removes stress" (n = 30, 50 per cent), and "choir enhances my intelligence" (n = 44, 73.3 per cent). We can attribute the positive perceptions of choral learning of the participants in school 1 to the presence of choices in choir participation, learning pace, and rich choral contents and flexible structures. Future studies should explore these aspects further.

In line with the aspiration of holistic education, choral education can serve as an additional outlet for group therapy, meeting the needs of students, providing them with the freedom of emotional expression, social support, and cognitive management skills. Group therapy in the informal choral setting can provide opportunities for emotional experiencing, self-expression, cathartic experience, social acceptance and support, guidance, and training in areas of social deficit (see also Shechtman, 2002). Future research should examine how the choir in the context of group therapy can promote students' wellness, enhance positive emotions, wisdom, health, and creativity.

CONCLUDING REMARKS

Our exploratory study suggested that the school as a system entails a specific and dynamic organisational culture. In adopting national policies and initiatives, schools impose their values and expectations that influence their students' perceptions and consequently, their quality of learning. The investigation of students' perceptions enlightens us on the inter-relations between external factors (e.g., schools' culture, organisation, and structure of curricula) and students' personal views (e.g., perception). With open-ended questions and direct classroom observations, items generated captured the essence of the learning environments from the communication styles of the students. The phrases and sentences were structured according to the style of expressions of Singaporean secondary school students. To develop a culture-sensitive questionnaire, the present exploratory study should be extended to a large number of secondary school students across streaming levels (e.g., express, normal academic, and normal technical). Similar surveys should be carried out in other CCA and non-CCA settings. A general questionnaire based on Singaporean educational philosophy, initiatives and policies, as well as classroom climates can be cross-validated with the existing learning environment questionnaires. Responses from open-ended questions (see Tables 4.3 and 4.4) confirmed and provided further perspectives to our findings in quantitative analysis. In line with the aspirations of holistic education, students should be engaged actively in co-forming their learning climate. Developing questions from the students' perspectives is one of the many ways. It can and should be accompanied by direct classroom observations and interventions, interviews and dialogues, to name a few.

NOTE

Permission is granted to include the paper "An exploratory study on Singapore's secondary school students' perceptions of choral learning" (by Ai-Girl Tan & Flora Yee) released in Asia Pacific Education Review, vol. 4, no. 2. Two tables (Tables 4.3 and 4.4) were added to the chapter to elaborate further students' views on choral learning. Minor editorial changes more introduced for ease of reading.

CHAPTER 5

Uncovering Children's Perceptions and Learning: Some Strategies

TAN AI-GIRL, LIM AI-HUA AND
TAN CHEE-YUEN

INTRODUCTION

A classroom is defined as a *space* for any form of beneficial, ethical and realistic experience. Learning is experiential, contextual and cultured. Hence, spaces for learning can be constructed physically, interpersonally and mentally. The physical spaces for learning include the classroom, library, music room, science laboratory, gymnasium, and school canteen. The interpersonal spaces for learning can be constructed when two or more persons with a similar motive collaboratively acquire knowledge or skills, problem solve, discover new ways of life, and play. Our minds construct the (perceptual) world in which we live. In solving everyday problems, for instance, the learners experience recursive mental processes, in problem finding, redefinition of problem, generation of possible means, selection of the best strategies, implementing them, and finally reviewing, reflecting and evaluating the problem solving phases. Mental spaces are "constructed," "free," "adjusted" to "accommodate" these cognitive processes to take place "simultaneously" and/or "in a recursive, or cyclic manner." In everyday classrooms, learning spaces are constructed through selected activity structures such as reading, writing, games, group discussion, debate, role-play, reading, writing, and web-search. A computer- or multimedia-based classroom creates virtual space of learning. The canteen and sport-field provide the space for learning social skills.

According to hybridity theory, people in a given community draw on multiple resources or funds to make sense of the world, and in our work, to make sense of oral and written texts. Hybridity is about "integration of competing knowledge and discourses to the texts one reads and writes, to the space, contexts, relationships one encounters, and to a person's identity enactments and sense of self." (Moje et al, 2004: 42) "Knowledge is the full utilisation of information and data coupled with the potential of the people's skills, competencies, ideas, intuitions, commitments and motivation." (Gupta et al, 2004: 4) According to Gupta and colleagues (2004), knowledge presents in ideas, judgments, talents, root causes, relationships, perspectives and concepts. It is stored in a person's head (tacit) or is codified and expressed as information in databases, documents, products, services, facilities and systems (explicit). "A discourse is a configuration of knowledge and its habitual forms of expression, which represents a particular set of interest." (The New London Group, 1996: 75)

Knowledge and discourse draw from different spaces: the first spaces being people's home, community and peer networks, the second being formalised institutions such as work, school, and temple or church, and the third being the "in-between" (Bhabha, 1994:1) or hybrid space. In the third or hybrid space one may experience oppositional categories of knowledge and discourses work together to generate knowledge, new discourses and new forms of literacy. In this space, several different funds of knowledge and discourse can be both productive and constraining in terms of one's literate, social, and cultural practices and ultimately one's self development. The third space (Gutierrez et al, 1999) can be a scaffold used to move students through zones of proximal development toward better honed academic and school knowledge. It can be regarded as a navigational space, a way of crossing and succeeding in different discourse communities. Or it is where everyday and academic knowledge and discourses are challenged and new knowledge are generated. Learning involves among others knowledge transformation (Gupta et al, 2004):

- socialisation (from tacit to tacit), where individuals acquire new knowledge directly from others;
- externalisation (tacit to explicit), where the articulation of knowledge into tangible form through dialogue;
- internalisation (explicit to tacit) such as learning by doing, where the individuals internalise knowledge from documents into their

own body of experience; combination (explicit to explicit), different forms of explicit knowledge are combined such as that in documents or on databases.

"Experience is realistic, not abstract." Dewey (1884: 289) Children's perceptions represent their state of understanding and socio-cultural experiences. It is a meaningful act to uncover children's perceptions of social phenomena or persons as it likely elicits information about children's preference, desire, will and experience. In school, children and teachers are in an interdependent learning and teaching relation. Children are social actors and partners in learning and teaching. Teachers are predecessors, socialising agents, and creativity agents for children (see Simonton, 1975); they are key socialisation agents after parents. As such, in any educational reform it is important to take children's experiences and socio-cultural diversity into consideration (Nieto, 1994). Any effort to facilitate creativity and goodness in school settings must take into account the roles of the teacher, who is called to realise the goals specified by national curricula and educational programmes (see Diakidoy & Kanari, 1999). Any effort to facilitate creativity and goodness in schools must also take into the account the children, who are the partners and clients of teaching and learning.

Are children competent in assessing activities they like? Research on pupils' self-assessment of competencies (e.g., Stipek & MacIver, 1989; Cole et al, 1997) showed that children are able to convey their competency beliefs and assess the usefulness and importance of various learning activities (e.g., mathematics, music and sport) (Wigfield et. al, 1997). By grade 4 (age: 9–10 years), children would have developed a stable and consistent set of beliefs about themselves, their general beliefs about cognitive ability and their ability to exert control over performance (Bouffard & Vezeau, 1998). They would be able to make self-appraisals of their capabilities (Bouffard, 1998). In fact, children in the age range of 9 to 12 years show a pattern of brain activation in a spatial working memory task that is remarkably similar to that of adults (Nelson et al, 2000). Pupils are partners in learning and teaching. Their perceptions, experiences and expectations should be considered in any educational reform (Nieto, 1994). Pupils' views of desirable activities entail numerous connotations. Referring to their views, we know the kinds of activities they enjoy, experience, and are able to manage.

THE STUDY

This chapter reports on the second author's experience in eliciting children's views and integrating them into teaching and learning. Specifically, the focus of the discussion was on three innovative teaching strategies: brainstorming in process writing, the 3-2-1 strategy, and challenge corner.

The Teacher

The second author was in her early twenties and was a third year student of a four-year Bachelor degree program. During the study, she was attached to the school as a trainee teacher undertaking a two-month teaching practice programme (between February and April 2004). Volunteering as a Sunday school teacher, she displayed multiple competencies in managing classroom and in helping children with learning difficulties. During teaching practice, she taught the English language, mathematics and social studies. Overseeing her performance were a teacher educator (the first author), a co-operating teacher (or the class teacher), and a senior mentor from the school. The school personnel and the teacher educator supervisor agreed that she out-performed her contemporaries in several ways including competence in designing effective learning activities, examination questions, and creative learning tools. She took the initiative to prepare comprehensive lesson plans and to consciously make reference of works of other teacher educators. In addition, she sought advice from other teacher educators for some of her self-designed activities. Included into her lesson plans were rationales of teaching, reflections of learning process and outcome, and her views of cultivating creativity.

The School Culture

The school to which the second author was attached underwent an innovative and structural transformation. Under the leadership of a new principal, the school introduced several measures to integrate new educational initiatives. This included, the school encouraging beginning teachers to share their insight into and reflection on innovative and caring teaching and learning strategies. In general, the teachers worked diligently to ensure that the school met the expectation of a new validation model:

the School Excellence Model. The school believed in nurturing multiple talents and did not disregard new ideas brought forth by beginning teachers. Backing up with the dedicated school mentor and cooperating teachers, from the feedback of the trainee teachers, the school to a great extent gave them ample spaces to grow and to employ new teaching strategies.

The Children

Thirty-eight elementary school children's written works were analysed and discussed. Criteria for selection of their works were as follows: (1) The teacher did not encounter difficulty in collecting all children's learning responses as evidence of her teaching, (2) the availability of learning outcomes for a series of lessons on the same theme, and (3) the collection of the children's evidence of learning did not affect children's learning processes. The children were on average 12 years old. According to the report of the teacher, the children were spontaneous and helpful. Some of them might be shy to answer questions individually. They needed coaching for vocabulary and writing. There were two Asian international pupils in the class. One of them was not fluent in the English language, the main medium of instruction.

STRATEGIES TO ELICIT CHILDREN'S VIEWS AND LEARNING

Three strategies developed by the second author are discussed here. The strategies are integrated brainstorming, the 3-2-1 strategy and challenge corner. The strategies were integrated into lessons she taught during the first author's (also the teacher educator supervisor) formal observation.

Integrated Brainstorming

It was a challenging task to combining brainstorming, brain-writing (i.e., writing down ideas freely), and group work in lessons. To ensure that the children acquired multiple skills within a few hour lessons, the teacher had to be innovative to relate her teaching to the children's experiences, and to use their experiences as teaching resources. Writing composition was not an easy task for the Singaporean children whose everyday language was not the English language. To relate to new learning, the teacher of the study employed a multi-tasking lesson conducted in five-period lessons (each period lasted for thirty minutes). Here is an overview of the total number of lessons for process writing.

Lesson 1: Two periods:
    Brainstorming: Vocabulary, ideas and text type

Lesson 2: Two periods:
    First draft after group writing and group presentation
    Homework: Second draft - individual writing

Lesson 3: One period:
    Third draft: Final product

Briefly, in the first two periods, the teacher elicited the children's prior learning. They were exposed to slides of an overseas school downloaded from the website. Then, they were guided to an activity—brainstorming. Principles of brainstorming were introduced such as no criticism and non-judgmental. Thereafter, the children sat in-group to elicit their ideas about an ideal school. Roles of group members were assigned clearly, such as leader, recorder, and presenter. Time allocation was specified distinctly. The children moved into groups after the teacher clarified her expectations related to the task, behaviour, and time. Materials were distributed soon after. A self-designed worksheet was given to each group: My writing plan. The children brainstormed in 15–20 minutes an aspect of an ideal school that they wanted to write about, and elicited three ideas for that aspect. Based on the points brainstormed, they then outlined a paragraph (see appendix 5.1 for the group writing plan). Evaluation was conducted using the 3-2-1 strategy (see below) on learning outcomes of the lessons (see appendix 5.2 for the evaluation form).

As follow-up lessons, the children referred to the points they brainstormed and drafted an essay on "My ideal school." Three drafts were sent to the teacher. According to the objectives of the chapter, the teacher set criteria of assessment, i.e., text type structure (sub-headings), ideas of the pupils (essay contents), and grammar (future tense).

In the third and fourth periods, referring to the first drafts of the children the teacher focused on the structure of the essay, if it included introduction, sub-headings, and conclusion, the main content of the lesson. As homework, the children wrote the second drafts. The teacher enhanced the children's competence in organising structures and clarifying doubts in writing proper sentences. Finally, in the fifth lesson, referring to the third draft, the teacher focused on children's correct use of tenses. The theme selected was relevant to the children's experiences.

The following reports a two-period lesson in which the children experienced an integrated brainstorming and attended to group writing.

Tuning-in (10 minutes)

The *first ten minutes* was termed as the engaging period. The teacher related the topic of the lesson on "My Ideal School" to that on Singapore's education, a previous lesson of social studies taught to the same class. She highlighted the aspect of Singapore schools in the past and at the present. In addition, the children recapitulated scenes of their parents' schooldays and experiences. Explicitly the teacher alerted children of the possible links between today's lesson and that of the social studies. Thereafter, she showed the children a short video clip on how children in the United States learned. The two international children in the class were invited to share their education systems and school facilities. The teacher then informed the class of the lesson objectives and flashed the objectives (she termed it our mission) on the PowerPoint slide. She paused and asked if the children were ready for the lesson.

Instruction: The Theme (10 minutes)

In *the next ten minutes*, the teacher clarified the key term: "ideal." She asked the children to voice out their views of the term and what did the term mean to them. She elicited responses from the children:

> What do you understand by the term "ideal?"
> Why do you think that an ideal school is important?
> What comes to your mind when you hear the words "ideal school?"

To ensure that the task was meaningful to the children, the teacher invited the children to think about the need for an ideal school. She believed that by so doing the children would be able to set their mind for the task. Shortly after that the teacher facilitated an integrated brainstorming. The integrated brainstorming comprised the following steps:

- The class called out their views freely on "my ideal school."
- The teacher wrote down the children's ideas on the whiteboard using a semantic web. The semantic web helped the children to organise their ideas and build up their vocabulary. It was a graphic organiser with a bubble (or circle) in the centre and lines extended from the bubble to different directions for new ideas or vocabulary. As the children elicited their responses, the teacher started to add the ideas to the semantic web. The teacher encouraged the children to suggest possible subheadings to categorise the responses if the responses needed to be placed under different categories. The activity helped to develop children's the sense of ownership in their work.
- The teacher introduced text type structure (information text).
- The group brainstormed, wrote a paragraph and shared their writing with the class.
- The children were reminded of the importance to feel free to voice their ideas.

Instruction: The Information Text (10 minutes)

A sample "foxes" was used to introduce systematically the structure of information text, namely, the title, general statement, development and conclusion. The teacher engaged the children to make sense of learning. Together with the children, she explained the purpose of having a title. She highlighted "development" as part of the basic structure of information text and described the function of it. The teacher then revealed that the concluding paragraph was to summarise the writing. Lastly, the teacher prompted the children to think of how information can be organised and presented in the text. The teacher summarised the structure of the text for the class. The following were the conversational sentences to engage the children during lesson delivery.

- The part of the structure of information text includes the development portion, a series of paragraphs describing the subject.
  - For this text, which part do you think is the development portion?
- Can this paragraph come after the third paragraph?
- Now that we have an idea of what we can write in our essay, let's take a look of how to structure our writing using the format of informational text type. We take a look at a sample text.
- What do we have here? (Title)

- Why do you think it is necessary to have a title? (Tell the readers what the report is about)
- How can we introduce the different aspects of our ideal school systematically? (Sub-heading)
- What did the author used here to achieve the goal? (Sub-heading)

To provoke thinking, the children reflected independently upon the purpose of each feature in this text type structure. The teacher attempted to reveal the structure of the text type step by step to help the children organise their thoughts in small chunks.

Brainstorming (20 minutes)

The teacher gave instructions for group work. In groups, the children were to write a paragraph on a selected aspect of their ideal school. They were asked to use the graphic organiser and paragraph outline to guide their writing.

"Now, in your teams, select a particular aspect of the school and use the graphic organiser and skeleton to write a paragraph on the aspect."

The teacher reminded the children of their roles and clearly elicited procedures of the task and time frame. She spent a couple of minutes to allow the children to ask questions to clarify any doubts they had. The children were assigned to different roles in a group. The teacher named the roles in such a way that all of them felt respected: the speed captain, super supporter, super recorder, synergy guru or chief of wacky ideas. She also elicited exemplified behaviour for each role. The following is the information of the group members' roles and descriptive responsibilities. Numbers in brackets indicated the number of children.

Speed captain (1): The speed captain keeps track of time factor. He/She also controls noise level of the group. The speed captain encourages the group by saying that "let's get more ideas," "let's come out with more views," and "let's move forward."

Super supporter (1): The super supporter makes sure all ideas are encouraged with no evaluation of idea. The super supporter encourages the group by saying, "all ideas are great" and "another fantastic idea."

Super recorder (1): The super recorder is responsible for taking note ideas on a piece of paper and placing it on a table for all to see.

Synergy guru (1): The synergy guru encourages the team mates to build on each other's ideas, by saying that "let's combine these two ideas."

Chief of wacky ideas (2): Having many wacky ideas sets the tone of creativeness and the possibility to increase the range of ideas. The chief of wacky ideas may say, "let's have a wacky idea." One of the chiefs will present the ideas on behalf of the group.

Note: The group with seven members will have two synergy gurus.

The teacher interacted with the children to observe (the children's facial expressions, postures and dialogues) how they worked and to provide them necessary scaffolding or suggestions. She gave a reminder five minutes before the time was up. The children were then asked to share the outcomes with the class. The children who did not present were encouraged to think of possible inputs for the presented paragraph. "Is there any thing that we can add to this paragraph?"

Lesson Closure (10 minutes)

In the *last ten* minutes, the teacher concluded the lesson by reviewing with the class what they learnt today. The teacher flashed the objectives and then asked the class if they accomplished the lesson objectives. "Have we accomplished our mission, what we have planned to do today?" The review helped the children to organise their thoughts. Thereafter, she assigned homework to the class by asking the children to work on their first draft for their writing based on the text type format and vocabulary they had learnt. They were encouraged to refer to additional vocabulary. The children were asked to choose three aspects to write on as the word limit for essays in PSLE requirement was between 150 and 250 words. A graphic organiser on the structure of an essay skeleton was distributed to guide the children in their writing. The teacher flashed the homework instructions on the PowerPoint slide to cater to the visual learners. Reflection plays a very important part in learning. Finally, the teacher requested the children to do a reflection using the 3-2-1 strategy. By doing reflection the children might get a better understanding of the lesson contents, and the learning process. Reflection can serve as feedback to the teacher on the children's learning

The 3-2-1 Strategy

Using the 3-2-1 strategy, after a lesson, the children were requested to spend a couple of minutes to elicit if they understood the contents, if they enjoyed the lesson (content related and/or others) and if they had any doubts (see appendix 5.2 for an example of the 3-2-1 strategy). On an A4-size paper, the following three phrases were included:

Three things I learnt after the lesson:
Two interesting things during the lesson:
One question I have after the lesson:

Flexibly, the teacher can modify the strategy to request the students to write instead of one but more questions, such as "questions I have after the lesson." Often a Likert-scale was employed to find out the students' reception of the lesson. In a lesson on "per cent," in addition to the 3-2-1 strategy the following item was included.

How did I feel when the teacher

- used the square grid to talk about fractions and per cent,
- asked you to observe the patterns such as between 9 % and 9/100, and
- asked you to convert fractions to percent and percent to fractions.

A four-point Likert scale was employed to elicit responses from the children. Symbols such as smiling face, normal face, and sad face were employed to indicate children's feelings corresponding to the three tasks above. Phrases to describe the feelings were included to ensure that the children shared the same connotations of the scale:

- I can understand it and I am happy.
- Sometimes I can do it, sometimes I cannot, but I learned after that.
- I do not know what to do and how to do.
- I do not know or understand what the teacher wants and teaches.

Challenge Corner

As a group or homework, the children were requested to attend to the task under a special session entitled the "Challenge Corner." The activity aimed to find out if the children master content knowledge by asking them to design a quiz question for their friend. The "Challenge Corner" was introduced in after group work and homework. The children first attended to the content related questions designed by the teachers. Then, they were encouraged to attempt to task designated under the "Challenge

Corner" to generate questions related to the contents. An example of a task under the "Challenge Corner" is cited below:

The children learned the "Guess and Check" strategy and applied it to word problem sums. On an A4-size paper, the children attended to two problem sums. They must use the check and guess strategy to attend to the sums. Thereafter they should attempt to create a story sum to be selected for a quiz given to their friends.

"Create a story sum to quiz your friends. The story sum should require your friend to use the strategy 'Guess and Check' that we learned during the lesson. You are to provide the answer with all workings clearly to assist your friends who may face difficulties in solving the sum."

The task demanded the children to move from the state of learner to the state of teacher. They were motivated to come out with a sum and its accompanied solutions. The idea of including their sums for a quiz for the peer was motivating. Furthermore, it was fascinating to have the possibility to aid their peer's learning and to provide solutions.

Before the children received the challenge corner as an individual work, they were encouraged to attempt to it in a group. In a mixed ability class, the teacher included the "Challenge Corner" into the group worksheet, and encouraged those who completed group work ahead of others to try. The choice of doing "Challenge Corner" was optional. Encouraging phrases were employed to engage the children who tried it out during group work and as an individual task as homework. The challenge corner provided space for differentiated learning.

OUTCOMES OF CHILDREN'S VIEWS AND LEARNING

This session we report on the learning outcomes of children from the lessons on "My Ideal School" that incorporated the integrated brainstorming and the 3-2-1 strategy, and those from "Challenge Corner."

My Ideal School

What did the children wish to have? A total of six groups or thirty-seven children participated in the brainstorming session. One child was absent. They chose facilities or places (three groups), freedom (two groups) and assessment (one group) as the aspect of the ideal school they wanted to write about during the brainstorming session (see Table 5.1).

TABLE 5.1   Group brainstorming ideas

Aspect	Group	Ideas related to the aspect
Facilities	1	Upgrade canteen to five-star restaurant. Change music room to arcade. Introduce physical education lessons for all sorts of sports, e.g., bowling and swimming.
	2	Have escalator instead of having stairs. Include indoor basketball court and swimming pool. Upgrade canteen into five-star restaurant.
	3	Upgrade fitting room to gymnastic room. Change stairs to escalator. Fill hall with air-conditioning.
Freedom	4	We can wear what we want (home clothes). We can bring anything we want to school. Bring laptops instead of books. We can go anywhere we want during class lesson without permission.
	5	Every pupil wears home clothes but not uniforms. Use palmtop instead of books. Choose our favourite teacher and classmates.
Assessment	6	Open textbooks to do the test. Give a longer time limit. Have one test per year (annual). Test only one subject: the English language.

Facilities: The children's responses were relevant to the contemporary societies in Singapore, such as the use of information technological (IT) devices such as laptops and palmtops to write and read, air-conditioning and luxurious or comfortable corners for meals and entertainment. Most buildings in Singapore are equipped with elevators or escalators. In the school, the lift was reserved for visitors or people with disabilities. Classrooms, the canteen and school hall is ventilated with fans. Situated on the equator, Singapore's room temperature is on average 27 to 30 degrees Celsius. Nearly all households have at least one room that is air-conditioned. Also most of the shopping malls, theatres, restaurants, and public service buildings are air-conditioned. In school, the staff room and library, computer or other resource rooms in general are air-conditioned. The difference between the school and the general public and home environments could be one of the main factors to call for a change in some facilities.

Freedom: The children enlisted ways they could feel more contented with regards to physical appearance (without uniform, girls do not need to tie their hair), time for free activities (longer recess and time to do exercise), convenience (bringing handy electronic devices to replace heavy books), and choices (food, teacher and classmates). The children of the study elicited reasons for the claim. One group included into their one-paragraph writing, reasons for their wishful list. For instance, they believed that home made food is healthy than food in the canteen. The group supported their argument with the consequence of having unhealthy food, i.e., falling ill and getting overweight.

> "We can bring any home made food because the school's food is very unhealthy to eat. By doing so we could prevent ourselves from sickness and overweight."

Likewise, the group elicited the same reason for their appeal to have longer opening hours for the gymnasium room.

"For P.E. lesson we could play what we want as long as we exercise. The gymnasium must be open everyday for the overweight to exercise when they are free."

The children's responses reflected what they experienced in schools. All school age children in Singapore spend on average six to eight hours in schools (including travelling time and time for extra- or co-curricular activities). Children wear uniform of their respective schools, and have one to two meals in the school canteen. Under the healthy lifestyle program, children who are "overweight" have to attend extra physical exercise activities.

Assessment: The reason for just having one subject to be tested was to reduce stress caused by too many examinations. Children in the Singapore's schools in general attended frequently to different means of assessment. Examination stress has been an issue of concern as examination is used to differentiate learning competences and abilities of the children. Under the current streaming system, the children were grouped according to their competence in the English language, Mandarin and mathematics. A proposal to have broad based streaming is on the way. Until a new policy is implemented, schools at the current stage focus on high academic achievements.

The 3-2-1 Strategy

At the end of the two-period lesson on the "Ideal School," the children employed the 3-2-1 strategy to elicit general and specific feedback of learning. The 3-2-1 strategy was modified somewhat according to the contents of the lesson on the Ideal School.

- Three things I learnt
- How do I feel about the lesson? Why is it useful for me?
- In what way(s) can I improve on my own learning?
- Questions I have after the lesson

Three things I learnt: The children's responses for the mathematics lessons were focused on mastery of content knowledge. Their responses corresponded to the key concepts taught during the lessons. However, the children's responses for the English language lessons were broadened to social domains (see two exemplified responses below).

012: How to brainstorm? Learn to write composition. To do things as a group.

016: How to brainstorm? How does the school system run in America? How did schools look like in the olden days?

The teacher employed inter-subject approach to prepare the children for the new learning. As tuning in for the lesson on the "Ideal School," contents of social studies were referred to. Then, the children were showed some slides on school life in another country. A creative technique, i.e., brainstorming was integrated as an idea generation tool for group writing.

Feedback on brainstorming: Children could relate well to the theme, and found the new tool useful to guide them for writing composition. Phrases surfaced for the question on their feeling for the lesson on brainstorming and its usefulness are such as "I feel great ...," "I feel happy ...," and "Excellent!" The responses showed that the children were positive towards the brainstorming technique as they could learn how to write composition, work as a team, and being able to engage in social interaction:

003: I feel good. It makes me do something for the future.

004: I feel great about brainstorming. I think that it's useful because it makes your brain thinks.

008: Excellent! I can learn more.

015: I feel happy because it can help me to improve my thinking creatively.

020: Useful and interesting so that I can use the useful tips for other work in my future.

025: I feel very good, because I can write my composition.

032: I felt happy, wonderful and useful to me because I can imagine that school X (name of the child's school) is my ideal school and I can come to school to learn happily everyday.

Ways to improve learning: Thirty-five statements were collected from the children. One of them did not answer this question: In what way(s) can I improve my learning? Another child regurgitated the question without any meaningful input. From the thirty-four responses, more than two-thirds (n = 21, 62 per cent) of them were related to the category "effort," e.g., trying hard, reading more, and doing more assessment. Five of them (15 per cent) believed in modelling what the teachers said and did or by paying attention to what was taught. The others (23 per cent) suggested the use of brainstorming. Table 5.2 displays exemplified ideas of the three categories of ideas on ways to improve learning.

Further question: Twenty-seven children (82 per cent) wrote down questions they had after the lesson. One response was not relevant, and hence was disregarded for the analysis. Out off the 27 responses, nearly half (n =12, 44 per cent) were related to general concerns such as education system, how to learn better, self-improvement and PSLE. The others were related to core learning objectives and introductory or tuning in materials. Table 5.3 outlines some exemplified questions.

Challenge Corner

The children attended the lesson on problem sum and use the guess and check strategy to solve questions set by the teacher in the class and as homework. The 3-2-1 strategy was used to find out what they learnt (three things), interesting contents (two things) and doubts or questions (one thing). From the responses, most of them acquired the basic contents,

TABLE 5.2   Ideas on ways to improve learning (Examples)

Efforts (62 per cent)

007	Study independently. (effort)
008	By doing more thinking (effort)
021	We should practice more. (effort)
022	By learning different words. (effort)
029	By revising, reading notes and books. (effort)
033	I need to do revision. (effort)

Pay attention to teachers (15 per cent)

006	By recording what the teacher said. By writing notes. (imitation)
009	Understand and listen that I can improve. (pay attention)
017	Using what the teacher has to teach. (modelling)

Use of brainstorming (23 per cent)

005	I can think using the brainstorming of my ideal school. (applying)
015	I can improve my own learning using brainstorming. (applying)
016	Doing brainstorming in every composition. (applying)

---

and asked questions related to alternative means to solve the same problem, and if the contents were relevant for the Primary School Leaving Examination (PSLE).

As homework, the children attended two problem sums and suggested one. Thirty of them participated in coming out with one question and its accompanied solutions. The question would be used to set a quiz workout for the children. The children who came out with the question were able to propose answers to the question. Here are examples of the children's work:

Question 1:
There are spiders and chickens in the science room. The total number of legs for the two animals is 96 and the total number of heads is 24. How many spiders and chickens are there in the science room?

TABLE 5.3 Exemplified questions

General concerns	

001	What would the Minister of Education think of the ideal school? (system)
013	How can I improve myself more? (general)
029	How to improve or remember what teachers teach? (general)
030	During PSLE do we need to write sub-titles when we are writing composition? (general)
033	How can we do to make what essay better? (general)
034	Why does the composition is needed in my test? (general)
036	How could I further improve my English language? (general)

Core learning objectives and tuning in materials

002	What was the 'Ideal' that you have? (tuning in-contents)
004	I would like to learn more about social studies of children in the past. What is it like? (content-introductory)
024	What do the schools in other country have? (content-introductory)
005	Must we include all our ideas of brainstorming to the draft we write? (content-brainstorming)
016	What facilities in school do they have in America? (content-introductory)
020	Why all compositions must have all the introduction, conclusion, sub-heading? (content-core)
022	Why do we write substitute? (content-core)
027	Is it possible to have arcade in the school? (content-group brainstorming)
028	Do we need to do subtitle? (content-core)

Working

Spider	Chicken	Total
12	12	120
8	8	96

Solution: Three are 8 spiders and 16 chickens.

Question 2:
John and Mary have $14 altogether. They use all the money to buy apples and pears. Each apple costs 40 cents and each pear costs 50 cents. They have 31 pears and apples. How many pears and apples did they buy?

Working

Pear 50 cents	Apple 40 cents	Total $14
14	17	$7.00 + $6.80 = $13.80
15	16	$7.50 + $6.40 = $13.90
16	15	$8.00 + $6.00 = $14.00

Solution: They bought 16 pears and 15 apples.

From the teacher's reflections, we realise that the children were competent in working cooperatively. The children were able to complete in teams the exercises in the worksheets. They did peer teaching according to the teacher's instruction. Overall, the children were able to solve the problems in their assigned homework using the method taught in class. Reflecting upon the children's learning outcomes, the teacher realised that most children were able to answer the first question in the quiz but not the second question. It would have been better if she had gone through the questions in team worksheets before letting the children attempt the quiz. In addition, the second question could have been made slightly easier.

CONCLUDING REMARKS

The study of children's perceptions of learning was significant for Singapore's education. The past half a decade has seen the introduction of a series of new initiatives to promote excellence in teaching and learning and in every child's holistic development. Among the initiatives were the information processing master plan, national education (implanting sense of belonging) and the thinking schools and a learning nation framework (highlighting cultivating creativity, problem solving and critical thinking competence). Educator or teachers are empowered to take care of the total development and wellness of the pupils. Schools in turn, are to ensure that teachers' wellness is given considerate attention. School management and leaders are encouraged to put mechanisms in place (e.g., free fruit) to promote total wellness of pupils. The second author was in her upper secondary school years when these new initiatives were introduced in 1997. She joined the cohort of the beginning teachers where the initiatives were integrated into educational and curricular studies highlighting innovative pedagogies. Included into the assessment of her teaching practice was teacher competence to organise pupil-centred lessons, critical and creative pedagogical competence and positive professional attitudes. In 2003, new school curricula were introduced to Singapore's elementary schools. The new curricula encouraged pupils to acquire strategic learning tools such as graphic organiser, mind mapping, questioning, and problem solving. Teaching is thus beyond delivery of content knowledge. Teaching engages the teacher's willingness and competence to co-construct spaces of learning to cultivate children's meta-learning skills and competence.

TEACHER CONCEPTIONS OF CREATIVITY

The beginning teachers under the second author's supervision were exposed to three articles (Tan, 1998; Tan, 2003; Tan 2004) on creativity, and how to cultivate a learner-centred environment for fostering creativity. The second author included her views on creativity when she taught the lesson on the "Ideal School." That lesson was observed by the second author. The first author shared openly her conceptions of creativity. In her lesson plan, she posed two questions: What does creativity mean to me? How can I apply knowledge of creativity to my teaching? She iterated that there are many aspects of creativity. One of them is to allow children to voice their opinions freely (Tan, 1998: 9) in the context of exerting a *balance* between *freedom* and setting *boundaries*. According to her, "teachers would need to set a boundary. It is within this boundary that the pupils are encouraged to let their creative juices flow." Another aspect of creativity was to encourage children to *relate* learning in the classroom to their daily life or to other subjects that they have studied. By doing so the second author believes that children would learn to appreciate new knowledge.

During the tuning in session on the "Ideal School," the second author applied the two aspects of creativity, namely setting realistic boundaries for free expression and making experiential connections. Concretely, she invited the children to share freely their experiences during holidays.

In addition, the second author considered it important to guide children to *see the same thing or issue from different perspectives*. During the tuning in session on the "Ideal School," she invited the international children in the class to share their views on the education systems in their countries. Also, the children watched a short video clip session on how American children learned.

Finally, to the second author, creativity was about *provoking thinking*. To include this aspect into her teaching, she adopted an inquiry approach. She posed questions such as "why do you think so?" and "how do you go about completing a given task?"

In sum, the second author regarded teaching as a process to empower children to acquire academic knowledge, life skills and moral values so to enable them to become a complete person. To achieve this, a teacher needs to create an enriching, thinking and collaborative environment to engage the pupils to processes of learning.

Constructing Learning Spaces

We advocate the importance of uncovering children's views in learning. We claim that by considering children's views and learning experiences, teachers and children indirectly engage in co-constructing learning spaces effective for children's learning. Space like time is a concept of orientation, created by mankind. Space can be physical, interpersonal, social, intra-personal, and mental. Human relations contribute to the formation of learning spaces for collaboration, dialogue, negotiation, and other human relations-related activities. Two or more persons with the same intent may construct common spaces for a shared task and toward an agreeable goal. The concept of zone of proximal development (ZPD) can be regarded as an example of socially constructed space of learning and thinking. In this space, the experienced scaffolds the novice to solve a problem, or to acquire designated skills or knowledge. Bandura's vicarious reinforcement highlights engagement of the learner in correcting his/her own maladaptive behaviour (e.g., aggression). In this incident, the learner in an interpersonal "space" observes, models others and adjusts his/her behaviour. Lay people's conceptions of "spaces" include connotations of "opportunities for new experiences," "allowances for trial and error," "acceptance of mistakes," and "support for areas of improvement." This chapter outlines one example of classroom action research. The authors were action researchers. Working as a team, the authors who were a teacher educator, a teacher, and a graduate researcher were able to synergise their strengths to work out something meaningful for the children. Before the teacher started her attachment in school, she attended a pre-practicum meeting. In this meeting, which lasted for one hour, the teacher together with her peer learned to undertake their roles as a beginning teacher. Negotiation on teaching expectations was allowed to enable the beginning teachers to adjust and embark on potentially favourable and strong areas. Group work was encouraged to facilitate children-centred teaching and learning. Wellness of the teachers was stressed. In this manner, interpersonal spaces were co-constructed for the beginning teachers to try new strategies and to enjoy different experiences.

"Pedagogy is a teaching and learning relationship that creates the potential for building learning conditions leading to full and equitable social participation." (The New London Group, 1996: 60) In pedagogy of spaces, teaching and learning is in a relationship that focuses on co-constructing and expanding learning spaces for full and equitable social participation. An indispensable aim of teaching is to co-construct with children cognitive and emotional spaces that can embrace, assimilate and accommodate children's "lived experiences" (see Athey, 1990). To make learning meaningful for children, it is essential to empower children to take charge of their views and preferred and perceived useful activities. Pedagogy of spaces thus aims to build a child-centred teaching and learning relationship that allows children to participate in learning actively, meaningfully, and confidently. We claim that exploring children's perceptions and considering children's experiences and views is an effective means for teachers to identify and include children's familiar resources from different knowledge and discourse spaces (e.g., home, school and new forms of literacy). Engaging children in in-depth dialogues with experienced learners and experts may help children to move between their social-historical spaces of discourse to the in-between "hybrid" spaces of discourse that encourage knowledge innovation and creation.

Teaching includes the competence to evaluate learning outcomes. In addition to designing learning activities, a teacher should possess competence to evaluate children's learning outcomes, to find out if his/her teaching is effective. Evaluation includes giving immediate feedback to children with regard to their learning, and using the feedback from children (i.e., integrating children's views). In our study, the children learned to assess their learning through the 3-2-1 strategy. They first elicited what they learned, what they found as interesting, and query remaining after learning. This strategy allowed the children to give feedback and to assess their own learning. Teachers have to develop insights into exploring and uncovering evidence of learning in children's writing, questioning, and answers to their self-generated questions.

ACKNOWLEDGEMENTS

This chapter is dedicated to children of Yuhua Primary School. Talent is in the eye of the beholder. The authors expressed sincere thanks to Germaine Koh, Robin Ong, and Teneline Tay Choon-Eng for their openness and support for innovative teaching and learning.

APPENDIX 5.1   Group Writing Plan

Group members: _____   Date: _____

Write down an aspect of your ideal school that you wish to include in your composition.

My Writing Plan

An aspect of the ideal school that I want to write:

_____

Descriptions of my ideas:

Idea #1: _____

_____

Idea #2: _____

_____

_____

Idea #3: _____

_____

Other information: _____
(optional)

Great! Refer to the ideas and write a paragraph

Teacher user guide

How to use the organiser, My Writing Plan?

Help children to focus on one aspect of their ideal school. Guide them to generate ideas in a group. Encourage children to negotiate with their group members and to decide on one aspect of the school they wish to include to their writing. Children can write their ideas in any sequence. For example, they may choose to fill in the characteristic of 'facilities' before filling in the characteristic of 'freedom', or vice versa.

APPENDIX 5.2

(Feedback on the lessons on my ideal school)

- Three things I learnt from the lesson

- How do I feel about brainstorming? Why is it useful to me?

- In what way(s) can I improve on my own learning?

- Questions I have after the lesson:

APPENDIX 5.3

Paragraph Outline

Teacher user guide

The graphic organiser, Paragraph Outline, helps children to put systematically the information that they want to include into a paragraph. They may refer to the organised information as a draft for essay writing.

Epilogue

LEARNER-CENTRED STRATEGIES

Our chapters report studies that employed multiple methods to uncover children's views and to enhance children's learning. In all studies we first engaged action researchers to elicit their views of children and their conceptions of creative teaching. Action researchers who were graduates of the Masters programmes at the National Institute of Education were encouraged to audit modules on research methodologies. They were invited to present their studies at the local and international educational conferences. For all studies reported in this book, open-ended questions were first employed to uncover children's views. Referring to children's responses to open-ended questions, classroom observations, and literature reviews, the researchers designed a survey questionnaire to further uncover children's views in learning. The questionnaire was administrated with help of classroom teachers who were action researchers of the studies. As the questionnaires took into consideration views of children and teachers and referred to the contents of related literature, the reliabilities of the questionnaires were high (Chapters 1–4). The combined qualitative and quantitative methods enabled the researchers to have a distinct and comprehensive view of children's wishful activities. Incorporating their views into learning programs, children likely enjoyed and engaged in learning (see Chapters 3 and 5). We also introduced innovative tools such as the 3-2-1 strategy, brainstorming, and challenge corner (Chapter 5) with the intention to construct "hybrid spaces" for children to create new knowledge and to engage in new discourses. In sum, all the studies were learner-centred, exploratory, and somewhat design-based. Table E.1 summarises selected research methods and issues of concern.

Learner-centred strategies were employed in our studies to uncover children's views or perceptions of learning. In brief, learner-centred education (Tan, 1998) acknowledges that every child is unique in his/her learning and thinking styles. Every child has the potential to be competent in one or more learning domains. Teachers and children engage in frequent dialogues. Spaces are co-constructed through dialogues and open communications. In addition, children write journals daily on significant events and learning experiences, through which they may give feedback

TABLE E.1 Methods and issues in individual studies

Chapter	Methods	Issues
1	Open-ended questions to survey development Qualitative and quantitative	*Attended*: Gender difference, contextual equivalence and culture-specific to classroom learning activities, subject/thematic perspectives *Arising*: Female favoured routine activities.
2	Open-ended questions to survey development Qualitative and quantitative	*Attended*: Gender difference, contextual equivalence and culture-specific to characteristics of good teachers and interpersonal domains of learning *Arising*: Gender was not that plausible to cluster children according to their responses. Female responded highly to some items related to pedagogical competence and interpersonal dispositions.
3	Classroom experiences, design-based learning, and intensive teacher-student interactions. Mainly qualitative.	*Attended*: Relatively high iterations of getting children's responses and feedback, verbal and written, over a relatively long duration of interaction. Creative activities for children were facilitated.
4	Open-ended questions to survey development. Qualitative and quantitative.	*Attended*: Gender diversity, school diversity, and what secondary school students deemed as good for choral learning. *Arising*: Female students' ratings were higher than male students' ratings. Females liked co-operative and males liked competitive learning environments.
5	Classroom experiences, design-based learning, and intensive researcher-teacher- children interactions. Mainly qualitative.	*Attended*: Innovative teaching strategies. Some iterations of engaging children to evaluate and give feedback on learning.

of learning regularly to their teachers. Teachers systematically document their teaching materials and procedures, as well as students' learning processes, learning outcomes, and general and specific learning experiences with their peers. They value students' interactions, group or interpersonal dynamics, and personal learning difficulties. Special sessions are facilitated in-group or individually for children who have learning difficulties. Scaffolding is given to children who wish to face challenges and who are in need. Collaboration in the form of group and project works is facilitated to meet the needs of learning of individual children. Teachers in designing classroom activities and in selecting suitable learning materials, consider the individual child's experiences and socio-cultural backgrounds. The learner-centred approach to teaching focuses on how teachers empower the learners the responsibilities to acquire and apply knowledge and skills. It enhances the learners' motivation in and enjoyment of knowledge acquisition and innovation.

Four learner-centred strategies were employed.

Strategy 1: Expanding learning spaces

Moving beyond the conventional learning objectives that end at acquiring knowledge and skills, learner-centred education endorses knowledge creation and innovation. Design is regarded as an effective activity that engages learners in innovative and creative learning processes. In designing, one expands the spaces of learning and thinking. Teachers who engage in learner-centred and design-based education adopt learning paradigms that are ethical, caring, open, and innovative. Learning is multi-faceted, multi-disciplinary, and multi-level. In design-based and actor (or learner)-centred learning environments, the learners are the main persons who engage in knowledge and skill acquisition, application and innovation. They learn to be persistent in their aspirations, confident to challenge boundaries, and endured to withstand failures and mistakes. Teachers are facilitators, supporters, and challengers.

Strategy 2: Acknowledging children's constructive wishes

Children' views and perceptions are sources of information about what they like and dislike, what they have experienced, and what they perceive as positive, interesting and motivating. A pleasant learning environment can be constructed if the teacher considers children's preferences and wishes. Children are likely to commit themselves to learning, if their preferred learning styles and activities are considered and integrated into lessons. The learner-centred approach allows children to voice their opinions, share their views with peers and adults, and evaluate learning processes. Children are given the opportunity to learn independently and collaboratively.

Strategy 3: Exploring children's perceptions of usefulness and goodness

Fostering excellence in the classroom challenges the teachers' competence to select suitable learning activities, to enhance students' intrinsic motivation and self-confidence, and to provide opportunities for knowledge and skills acquisition. Students possess conceptions of usefulness and goodness for learning activities, teacher characteristics, and learning environments. Teachers should uncover students' perceptions of usefulness and goodness and should find out why some activities and people (i.e., teachers and peers) are less favourable, and some are well received. In designing learning activities, teachers should be creative and critical when they incorporate students' interests, predict constructive learning outcomes, and induce stimulating learning environments. The way an activity is introduced will affect students' perception of this activity and consequently the effectiveness of the learning processes.

Strategy 4: Identifying teacher roles

Teachers' beliefs, attitudes and educational philosophy influence their instructional approach, classroom climate and roles that they may adopt. Roles are people's functions, the parts taken by them in life or in any activity. It is the way in which they are involved, and the way they influence an activity or a situation. Teacher roles state the position that a teacher has in a society, in school and in the classroom, and ways they are expected to behave in a relationship with students and with other related persons. An individual with a "creative teacher" role-identity would like to engage in performances that are unconventional such as employing non-traditional texts and conducting innovative projects. A person can have more than one identity associated with a given role, and can have more than one role associated with a given identity. Teachers, for instance, can possess multiple identities such as being creative, friendly, caring, flexible, strict and serious. They can also have multiple roles attached to the creative identity. A teacher can be a creative classroom manager, a creative mentor, a creative administrator and a creative disciplinary master.

There are two important factors that support learner-centred education.

The first factor is related to a student's intrinsic motivation. Intrinsic forms of motivation lead to positive outcomes such as high level of creativity, more involvement in thinking, less drop-out, and better conceptual learning. The learners can be more interested in learning, if they are allowed to participate actively in the learning process. Intrinsic motivation varies as a function of one's feelings of competence and self-determination. When learners perceive that they have control over and responsibility for the learning processes, methods and strategies, they are likely to be committed to the task and thus be motivated to achieve.

The second factor is a student's self-determination (Deci & Ryan, 1985). Learners must believe that they are sufficiently competent in order to execute the actions that lead to achievement. When learners are self-regulated and self-determined, it is likely that their performance and motivation will increase. Perceived academic competence and self-determination influence intrinsic academic motivation positively, and have a positive impact on school performance. When students think that they are competent in a domain, it is likely that their intrinsic motivation will increase. The same outcome is reported when students possess high intrinsic motivation and self-esteem. Students' motivation can also be enhanced through the acquisition of cognitive and metacognitive strategies. These strategies give learners the competence to determine their learning outcomes. Through active participation, students build up the sense of ownership for any learning activities, a motivating force for effective learning.

SOME INSIGHTS

Our studies stimulated some insightful thoughts. First, in view of the importance of informed practice, we regard highly action research and teacher and student engagement in classroom-based studies. In a naturalist environment, we have to adopt open attitudes and use multi-methodologies. Teachers are encouraged and invited to participate as researchers, classroom instructors, and observers. They work closely with educator researchers and scientists in nationwide projects that collect best evidence-based practices. In such projects, teachers and researchers alike have to be ready to engage in meta-analyses, in inventing theories, in acknowledging multidimensional, multi-causal and multi-modal representations and in the use of information and communication technologies.

Second, classroom research challenges our wisdom to evaluate and reflect upon effectiveness of research and intervention programs. We thus not only adopt classroom culture, but also uphold ethics of research and humanity. Our studies and interventions should be beneficial for children's learning, growth and development. In addition, it is essential to ensure that our studies establish conceptual and contextual equivalence, and linguistic and cultural specificity and diversity (i.e., gender, school and ethnicity). Our studies showed that gender diversity is a fact of life. It exists in Singaporean classrooms. So do school cultural diversity and likely ethnic diversity. Learner-centred education has to embrace these diversities for the better growth of individual children. Differences can become strengths when they are well managed.

Third, learning in the knowledge- and information-communication technology based era is a principle of an organisation (Masschelien, 2001). Educators and teachers alike often face situations that challenge them to decide between different approaches of teaching influenced by social practices. Literacy education is an issue of concern. Literacy simply refers to reading and writing. In literacy education, one is interested in empowering the children the competence and confidence to "do" with texts intellectually and socio-culturally. "Texts" can be presented in print, hard bound, in electronic, or in human communication to oneself and to others. As everything is a text, we "read" and "write" our environment (Scott & Gough, 2003). Deeply, "texts" store human wisdom, intelligence, and socio-cultural practice. In literacy pedagogy, we engage children in individualised cognition: making sense of the texts, and constructing meaning from the texts for personal engagement in socio-cultural practices, as well as mediate self-transformation. Educators and teachers are challenged to decide between giving attention to children of diversified backgrounds (i.e., achievers, underachievers, gifted and children with special needs) and having standardised curricula for all. In coaching a class of 30–40 children (an average class size for a Singaporean primary school), educators may have to make a clear stand when to allow discovery learning and when to discipline children's behaviour. As a matter of fact, children at the end of the primary and secondary school years sit for national examinations that qualify them for certain choices of school and specialised areas. As such, learning in schools is beyond just knowledge and skill acquisition; it is a way to pave a child's future. When good grades remain a major benchmark for educational and career advancement, schooling entails connotations of social practices. Educational practice and pedagogy thus have to accommodate children's social and functional needs.

CONCLUDING REMARKS

What is education for children of the twenty-first century? How does schooling relate to education in the new world? Education must assist children in exploring and living in harmony in the world (Schantz & Rideout, 2003). The skills that the twenty-first century students needs are such as reading, listening, writing, teamwork, speaking, conflict resolution, leadership, computer literacy, decision-making, and personal responsibility (Sigworth et al, 2003). Information and communication technologies (ICT) competencies are incorporated in school curricula and as resources for teaching and learning (see Seng, 2003, for an example how IT skills are incorporated into the Singapore's primary schools). Various modes of thinking are essential (Goeker, 2003): reactive (at the event level), adaptive (patterns of events), creative (systemic structures in response to our shared visions and paradigms) and generative (paradigm or shared vision). The paradigmatic or shared vision is the most powerful leverage point for change. A vision is about what we desire. Vision shapes everything else. To create a just and sustainable future, it is essential to emphasise on creativity in the contexts of social actions, to strengthen freedom and civil liberties, and to teach more than one type of socio-economic systems. Education is for personal growth and is about the presence of real experiences in social worlds. Hence, education should be taken as a means to peace and war prevention, elimination of poverty and balancing ecology (Boyer, 2002). In the discourse of the learning society, learning takes place in environment, which offers resources and limitations. Learning is about the development and stimulation of the learning capacity, i.e., the learning competence or the capacity for labour and energy. Such a discourse may result in the loss of childhood. The discourse of the loss of childhood is concerned with building a capacity for questioning the self and making a judgment about the meaning of the needs of life (Masschelien, 2001). The new pedagogy should address the issue of the loss of childhood, i.e., to educate the "whole" child using the principles of continuity, adequacy, and completeness, taking the child's experience as pre-theoretical understanding, and play as appropriation to reality (Lamb, 2001). We have to ensure that children of the twenty-first century are not deprived of basic education, gender and other equalities, rights, health and happiness. Our book in its limited capacity examines some of the concerns from the perspectives of eliciting children's views in learning. We hope this book serves as a preliminary document for further dialogues and discourses on children's views in learning in Singapore and beyond.

References

PREFACE

Baltes, P. B., & Freund, A. M. (2003). Human strengths as the orchestration of wisdom and selective optimization with comprehension. In L. G. Aspinwall & U. M. Staudinger (Eds.), *A Psychology of Human Strengths: Fundamental Questions and Future Directions for a Positive Psychology* (pp. 23–35). Washington: American Psychological Association.

Baltes, P. B., Staudinger, U. M., & Lindenberger, U. (1999). Lifespan psychology: Theory and application to intellectual functioning. *Annual Review of Psychology*, 50, 471–502.

Global Population Profile (2002). World Health Organization: Highlight.

Ministry of Education (2004). *Educational Statistics Digest 2003*. Singapore: MOE, Management and Information and Research Branch Planning Division.

Pardeck, J. T. (2002). *Children's Rights: Policy and Practice*. New York: The Haworth Social Work Practice Press.

UNESCO (2000). Global Synthesis: Education for all 2000 Assessment in Dakar, Senegal April 26–28, 2000.

UNESCO (2003). UNESCO's Gender Mainstreaming Implementation Framework (GMIF) for 2002–2007 (http://www.unesco.org/women – September 2003).

UNESCO (2004). Third High-Level Group Meeting on Education for All in New Delhi November 10–12, 2003.

United Nations (2003). Population, Education and Development. New York: United Nations.

World Health Report (2003). Shaping the future. WHO: Healthy Environment for Children: http://www.who.int/features/2003/04/en/print.html accessed April 13, 2004.

World Population Prospects (2002). The 2002 Revision and World Urbanization Prospects: The 2001 Revision. http://esa.un.org/unpp, accessed April 13, 2004.

INTRODUCTION

Ainsworth, M. D. S. (1969). Object relations, dependency and attachment: A theoretical review of the infant-mother relationship. *Child Development*, 40, 969–1025.

Baltes, P. B. (1987). Theoretical propositions of life-span developmental psychology: On the dynamics between growth and decline. *Developmental Psychology*, 23(5), 611–626.

Baltes, P. B. (1997). On the incomplete architecture of human ontogeny: Selection, optimization and compensation as foundation of developmental theory. *American Psychologist*, 52(4), 366–380.

Beresin, A. R. (2002). Children's expressive culture in light of September 11, 2001. *Anthropology and Education Quarterly*, 33(3), 331–337.

Bolger, N., Davis, A., & Rafaeli, E. (2003). Diary methods: capturing life as it is lived. Annual Review of Psychology, 54, 579–616.

Bornstein, M. H. (2002). Toward a multiculture, multiage, multimethod science. *Human Development*, 45, 257–263.

Bowbly, J. M. (1969). *Attachment and Loss, Vol. 1: Attachment*. London: Hogarth Press.

Bowbly, J. M. (1973). *Attachment and Loss, Vol. 2: Separation, Anxiety and Anger*. London: Hogarth Press.

Bowbly, J. M. (1980). *Attachment and Loss, Vol. 3: Loss, Sadness and Depression*. London: Hogarth Press.

Briton, B., & Fujiki, M. (2003). Blending quantitative and qualitative methods in language research and intervention. *American Journal of Speech and Language Pathology*, 12, 165–171.

Bronfenbrenner, U. (1979). *The Ecology of Human Development*. Cambridge, M.A.: Harvard University Press.

Bruner, J. (1997). Celebrating divergence: Piaget and Vygotsky. *Human Development*, 40, 63–73.

Bruner, J. T. (1998). Science, brain fiction. *Educational Leadership*, November, 14–18.

Cahan, E. D. (1992). John Dewey and human development. *Developmental Psychology*, 28(2), 205–214.

Csikszentmihalyi, M. (1988) Society, culture and person: A systems view of creativity. In R. J. Sternberg (Ed.), *The Nature of Creativity* (pp. 325–339). New York: Cambridge University Press.

Dewey, J. (1884). The new psychology. In Boydston, J. A. (Ed.), *The Early Works of John Dewey*, 1882–1897 (vol. 1, pp. 48–60). Carbondale, Illinois: Southern Illinois University Press.

Dewey, J. (1913). Reasoning in early childhood. In Boydston, J. A. (Ed.), *The Early Works of John Dewey*, 1882–1897 (vol. 7, pp. 369–376). Carbondale, Illinois: Southern Illinois University Press.

Doi, T. (1973). *The Anatomy of Dependence*. New York: Kodansha.

Engel, G. (1977). The care of patients: Art or science? *The Johns Hopkins Medical Journal*, 140(5), 222–232.

Flavell. J. H. (1999). Cognitive development: children's knowledge about the mind. *Annual Review of Psychology*, 50, 21–45.

Frankl, V. (1969/1988). *The Will to Meaning: Foundations and Applications of Logotherapy*. New York: A Meridian Book.

Franzosi, R. (1998). Narrative analysis or why and how sociologists should be interested in narrative. *Annual Review of Sociology*, 24, 517–554.

Furnham, A. (1988). *Lay Theories: Everyday Understanding of Problem in Social Sciences*. England: Pergamon Press.

Honig, A. S. (1999). The amazing brain. *Scholistic Early Childhood Today*, March, 20–22.

Kamil, M. L. (2004). The current state of quantitative research. *Reading Research Quarterly*, Jan-Feb-Mar, 39(1), 100–106.

Kid, S. A. (2002). The role of qualitative research in psychological journals. *Psychological Methods*, 7(1), 126–138.

Le Doux, J. (1996). *The Emotional Brain*. New York: Simon & Schuster.

Lewis, B. (1995). Psychotherapeutic discourse analysis. *American Journal of Psychotherapy*, 49(3), 371– (11 pages, from Proquest.umi.com/pqdweb?TS=1050923032&RQT=309&CC=2&Dtp=1&Did, downloaded on April 21, 2003).

Lomax, R. G. (2004). Whither the future of quantitative literacy research? *Reading Research Quarterly*, Jan-Mar, 39(1), 107–112.

Marshall, C., & Rossman, G. B. (1989). *Designing Qualitative Research*. Newbury Park: Sage.

Maslow, A. H. (1943). A theory of human motivation. *Psychological Review*, 50, 370–396.

Much, N. (1995). Cultural psychology. In J. A. Smith, R. Harre & L.V. Langenhove (Eds.), *Rethinking Psychology* (pp. 97–121). London: Sage.

Ritchie, S. M., & Rigano, D. L. (2002). Discourses about a teacher's self-initiated change in praxis: Storylines of Care and Support. *International Journal of Science Education*, 24(10), 1079–1094.

Schwarz, N. (1998). Warmer and more social: recent development in cognitive social psychology. *Annual Review of Sociology*, 24, 239–64.

Sen, A. (2001). *Development as Freedom*. Oxford: Oxford University Press.

Simonton, D. K. (2003). Qualitative and Quantitative Analysis of Historical Data. *Annual Review of Psychology*, 54, 617–640.

Sternberg, R. J. (1985). Implicit theories of intelligence, creativity and wisdom. *Journal of Personality and Social Psychology*, 49, 607–627.

Sternberg, R. J., & Grigorenko, E. L. (2001). United Psychology.–*American Psychologist*, 56(12), *1069–1079*.

von Bertalanffy, L. (1933/1962). *Modern Theories of Development: An Introduction to Theoretical Biology*. New York: Harper & Brothers.

Walsh, K. (2003). Qualitative research: advancing the science and practice of hospitality. *Cornell Hotel and Restaurant Administration Quarterly*, 44(2), 66–74.

Wertsch, J. V., & Tulviste, P. (1992). L.S. Vygotsky and contemporary developmental psychology. *Developmental Psychology*, 28(4), 548–557.

CHAPTER ONE

Ashby, F. G., Isen, A. M., & Turken, A. U. (1999). A neuropsychological theory of positive affect and its influence on cognition. *Psychological Review*, 106(3), 529–550.

Bandura, A. (1978). The self-system in reciprocal determinism. *American Psychologist*, 33, 344–358.

Bedny, G. Z., & Karwowski, W. (2001). Activity theory as a basis for the study of work. *Ergonomics*, 47(2), 134–153.

Beverdorf, D. Q., Hughes, J. D., Steinberg, B. A., Lewis, L. D. & Heilman, K. M. (1999). Noradrenergic modulation of cognitive flexibility in problem solving. *Neuroreport*, 10(13), 2763–2767.

Bruner, J. S. (1987). *Actual Minds, Possible Worlds*. Cambridge: Harvard University Press.

Bruner, J. (1997). *The Culture of Education*. Cambridge: Harvard University Press.

Chapman, A. (2003). Reflections on a social semiotic approach to discourse analysis in educational research. In T. O' Donoghue & K. Punch (Eds.), *Qualitative Educational Research in Action: Doing and Reflecting* (pp. 152–176). London: RoutledgeFalmer.

Deci, E. L., & Ryan, R. (1991). A motivational approach to self: integration in personality. In R. Dienstbier (Ed), *Nebraska Symposium on Motivation: Perspectives on Motivation* (Vol. 38, pp. 237–288). Lincoln, NE: University of Nebraska Press.

Deci, E. L., Scheimann, L., Wheeler, L., & Hart, R. (1980). Rewards, Motivation and Self-esteem. *Educational Forum*, 44, 429–433.

Halliday, M. A. K. (1979). *Languages Social Semiotics: The Social Interpretation of Language and Meaning*. London: Edward Arnold.

Isen, A. M., Daubman, K. A., & Nowicki, G. P. (1987). Positive affect facilitates creative problem solving. *Journal of Personality and Social Psychology*, 52(6), 1122–1131.

Isen, A. M., Johnson, M. M., Mertz, E., & Robinson, G. F. (1985). The influence of positive affect on the unusualness of word association. *Journal of Personality and Social Psychology*, 48(6), 1413–1426.

Lange, G. W., & Adler, F. (1997). Motivation and achievement in elementary children. Paper presented at the Biennial Meeting of the Society for Research in Child Development (62nd, Washington, D. C., April 3–6).

Lemke, J. L. (1987). Social semiotics and science education. *The American Journal of Semiotics*, 5(2), 217–232.

Premack, D. (1965). Reinforcement theory. In D. Levine (Ed),–*Nebraska Symposium on Motivation* (pp. 123–180). Lincoln: University of Nebraska Press.

Tan, A. G. (1998a). An exploratory study of Singaporean primary pupils' desirable activities for English lessons. *Education Journal*, 26(1), 59–76.

Tan, A. G. (1998b). Exploring primary pupils' desirable activities in mathematics lessons. *The Mathematics Educator*, 3(2), 26–37.

Tan, A. G. (1998c). Singaporean children's views of desirable activities and useful activities for fostering creativity. *Educational Research Journal*, 13(2), 197–220.

Tan, A. G. (2001a). Elementary school teachers' perception of desirable learning activities: A Singaporean perspective. *Educational Researcher*, 43(1), 47–61.

Tan, A. G. (2001b). Singaporean teachers' perceptions of activities useful for fostering creativity. *The Journal of Creative Behavior*, 35(2), 131–148.

Weinstein, C. S. (1991). The classroom as a social context for learning. *Annual Review of Psychology*, 42, 493–525.

CHAPTER TWO

Amabile, T. M., & Hennesy, B. A. (1987). *Creativity and Learning*. Washington, D. C: National Education Association.

Astington, J. W. & Barriault, T. (2001). Children's theory of mind: How young children come to understand that people have thoughts and feelings. *Infants and Young Children*, 13(3), 1–12 (Aspen Publishers, Inc.).

Barenboim, C. (1977). Developmental changes in the interpersonal cognitive system from middle childhood to adolescence. *Child Development*, 52, 129–144.

Beishuizen, J. J., Hof, E., van Putten, C. M., Bouwmeester, S., & Asscher, J. J. (2001). Students' and teachers' cognitions about good teachers. *British Journal of Educational Psychology*, 71, 185–201.

Bergreen, G. (1998). *Coping with Difficult Teachers*. New York: Rosen.

Bjorklund, D. F. (1999). Comment: what individual differences can teach us. In F. E. Weinert & W. Schneider (Eds.), *Individual Development from 3 to 12: Findings from the Munich longitudinal study* (pp. 29–37). Cambridge: Cambridge University Press.

Bouffard, T., Markovits, H., Vezeau, C., & Boisvert, M. (1998). The relation between accuracy of self-perception and cognitive development. *British Journal of Educational Psychology*, 68(3), 321–330.

Caspi, A. (2000). The child is father of the man: Personality continuities from childhood to adulthood. *Journal of Personality and Social Psychology*, 78(1), 158–172.

Cropley, A. J. (1992). *More Ways than One: Fostering Creativity*. Norwood, NJ: Ablex.

Cropley, A. J. (1997). Fostering creativity in the classroom: general principles. In M.A. Runco (Ed.), *The Creativity Research Handbook* (pp. 83–114). New Jersey: Hampton Press Inc.

Dacey, J. S. (1989). Discriminating characteristics of the families of highly creative adolescents. *The Journal of Creative Behavior*, 263–271.

Diakidoy, I. A. N., & Kanari, E. (1999). Student teachers' beliefs about creativity. *British Educational Research Journal*, 25(2), 225–241.

Eccles, J. S. (1999). The development of children ages 6 to 14. *When School is Out*, 9(2), 30–44.

Esquivel, G. R. (1995) Teacher behaviours that foster creativity (Special issue: Toward an educational psychology of creativity). *Educational Psychology Review*, 7(2), 185–202.

Fryer, M., & Collings, J. A. (1991) British teachers' views of creativity. The *Journal of Creative Behavior*, 75–81.

Furman, E. (1990). What is a good teacher? *Instructor*, p. 18.

James, A., & James, A. L. (2000). Childhood: Toward a theory of continuity and change. *The Annals of the American Academy*, 575, 25–36.

Jules, V., & Kutnik, P. (1997). Student perceptions of a good teacher: the gender perspective. *British Journal of Educational Psychology*, 67, 497–511.

Kutnik, P., & Jules, V. (1993). Pupils' perceptions of a good teacher: a developmental perspective from Trinidad and Tobago. *British Journal of Educational Psychology*, 63, 400–413.

Livesley, W. J., & Bromley, D. M. (1973). *Person Perception in Childhood and Adolescence*. London: John Wiley.

McLeod, J., & Cropley, A. J. (1989). *Fostering Academic Excellence*. Elmsford, NY: Pergamon Press.

McIntyre, T., & Battle, J. (1998). The traits of "good teachers" as identified by African-American and White students with emotional and/or behavioral disorders. *Behavioral Disorders*, 23(2), 134–142.

Miazzga, J. (2000). Development theories: it's time to review. *TCA Journal*, 28(1), 4–10.

Nelson, C. A., Monk, C. S., Lin, J., Carver, L. J., Thomas, K. M., & Truwit, C. L. (2000). Functional neuroanatomy of spatial working memory in children. *Developmental Psychology*, 36(1), 109–116.

Peevers, B. H., & Secord, P. F. (1973). Developmental changes in attribution of descriptive concepts and to persons. *Journal of Personality and Social Psychology*, 27, 120–128.

Piaget, J. (1962). *Play, Dreams and Imitation in Childhood*. London: Routledge & Kegan Paul.

Raslinda R., & Tan, A. G. (2003). Children's Perceptions of a Creative Teacher. Paper presented at the Asia Pacific Conference on Education (June 2–5). Singapore: National Institute of Education.

Selman, R. L. (1980). *The Growth of Interpersonal Understanding*. New York: Academic Press.

Selmon, R. L., & Byrne, D. F. (1974). A structural-developmental analysis of levels of role-taking in middle childhood. *Child Development*, 45, 803–806.

Stein, M. I. (1974). *Stimulating creativity: Vol. I- individual procedures*. New York: Academic Press.

Sternberg, R. J. (1985). Implicit theories of intelligence, creativity and wisdom. *Journal of Personality and Social Psychology*, 49, 607–627.

Sternberg, R. J. (1996). Investing in creativity: Many happy returns. *Educational Leadership*, 53(4), 80–84.

Stipek, D., & MacIver, D. (1989) Developmental change in children's assessment of intellectual intelligence. *Child Development*, 60, 521–538.

Tan, A. G. (1997). Educator roles in promoting creative thinking. *Jurnal Pendidikan Tinggi*, 4, 77–84.

Torrance, E. P., & Meyers, R. E. (1972). *Creative Learning and Teaching*. New York: Dodd, Mead & Co.

Treffinger, D. J., Ripple, R. E., & Dacey, J. S. (1968). Teachers' attitudes about creativity. *Journal of Creative Behavior*, 9, 269–274.

William, J. (1981). The perception of "things". In F. Burkhardt & F. Bowers (Eds.), *The Works of William James: the Principles of Psychology* (Vol. 2, pp. 722–775). Cambridge: Harvard University Press.

Zajonc, R. B. (1965). Social facilitation. *Science*, 149, 269–274.

CHAPTER THREE

Amabile, T. M. (1983). *The Social Psychology of Creativity*. New York: Springer.

Amabile, T. M. (1996). *Creativity in Context*. Colorado: Westview Press.

Beck, J. (1999). *How to Raise a Brighter Child*. New York: Pocket Books.

Bloom, B. (1985). On talent development (conversation between Ronald S. Brandt and Benjamin Bloom). *Educational Leadership*, September 1985, 33–35.

EL, CPDD (2003). Briefing by the English Unit, Curriculum Planning and Development Division, Ministry of Education (MOE, November 11) on New English Syllabus at MOE Building, Buona Vista.

Cropley, A. J. (1992). *More Ways than One: Fostering Creativity*. Norwood, NJ: Ablex.

Cropley, A. J. (1997). Fostering classroom creativity. In M.A. Runco (Ed), *The Creativity Research Handbook* (vol. 1, pp. 83–114).Cresskill, NJ.: Hampton Press.

Dewey, J. (1938/2002). *Experience and Education*. New York: Touchstone.

Dianaros A. M., Tan, A. G., & Soh, K. C. (2003). Enhancing children's creativity: An exploratory study on using the Internet and SCAMPER as creative writing tools. *The Korean Journal of Thinking and Problem Solving*, 13(2), 67–81.

Downing, J. P. (1997). *Creative Teaching: Ideas to Boost Student Interest*. Colorado: Press Englewood.

Esquivel, G. R. (1995). Teacher behaviors that foster creativity (special issue towards an educational psychology of creativity). *Educational Psychology Review*, 7(2), 185–202.

Gardner, H. (1983). *Frames of Mind: The Theory of Multiple Intelligences*. New York: Basic Books.

Goh, C. K. (1997). Shaping our future: Thinking schools and learning nation. *Speeches*, 21(3), 12–20.

Houtz, J. C. (1994). Creative problem solving in the classroom: contributions of four psychological approaches. In M. A. Runco (Ed.), *Problem Finding, Problem Solving and Creativity*. New Jersey: Ablex Publication Corp.

Jalongo, M. R. (2003). The child's right to creative thought and expression. *Childhood Education*, Summer, 218–227.

Rosenthal, R. Baratz, S., & Hall, C. M. (1974). Teacher's behaviour, teacher's expectations, and gains in pupils' rated creativity. *Journal of Genetic Psychology*, 124, 115–121.

Soh, K. C. (2000). Indexing creativity fostering teacher behaviour: A preliminary validation study. *Journal of Creative Behavior*, 34(2), 118–134.

Swartz, R., & Parks, S. (1994). *Infusing the Teaching of Critical and Creative Thinking into Elementary Instruction*. Pacific Grove, C.A.: Critical Thinking Press & Software.

Tan, A. G. (2000). *Psychology of Cultivating Creativity*. Singapore: Lingzi.

Templeton, S. (1991). *Teaching the Integrated Language Arts*. Boston: Houghton Mifflin Co.

Torrance, E.P. (1972). Can we teach children to think creatively? *Journal of Creative Behaviour*, 6, 114–143.

Walberg, H. J. & Stariha, W.E. (1992). Productive human capital: Learning creativity and eminence. *Creativity Research Journal*, 5, 323–341.

Zuckerman, M. (1977). *Scientific Elite: Nobel Laureates in the U.S.* New York: The Free Press.

CHAPTER FOUR

Anderson, G. J., & Walberg, H. J. (1972). Class Size and the social environment of learning: A mixed replication and extension. *Alberta Journal of Educational Research*, 18, 277–286.

Bauer, F. (1984). *Dateanalyses mit SPSS* (data analysis with SPSS). Berlin: Springer - Verlag.

Brekelmans, M., Wubbels, T., & Brok, P. (2002). Teacher experience and the teacher-student relationship in the classroom environment. In Goh, S. C., & Myint, S. K. (Eds.) *Studies in Educational Learning Environments: An International Perspective* (pp. 73–99). Singapore: World Scientific Publishing.

Byrne, D. B, Hattie, J. A., & Fraser, B. J. (1986). Student perceptions of preferred classroom learning environment. *Journal of Educational Research*, 81, 10–18.

Cortine, J. M. (1993). What is coefficient alpha? An examination of theory and application. *Journal of Applied Psychology*, 78, 98–104.

Dorman, J., Fraser, B., & McRobbie, C. (1994). Rhetoric and Reality: a Study of Classroom Environment in Catholic and Government Secondary Schools. Paper Presented at the Annual Meeting of the American Educational Research Association, New Orleans, Louisiana, April.

Doyle, W. (1979). Making managerial classrooms. In D. Duke (Ed.), *Classroom Management* (pp. 42–74) (78ᵗʰ Yearbook of the National Society for the Study of Education, Part 2). Chicago: University of Chicago Press.

Fisher, D. L., & Waldrip, B. G. (1997). Cultural factors of science classroom learning environments, teacher-student interactions and student outcomes. *Research in Science and Technology Education*, 17(1), 83–96.

Fisher, D. L., & Waldrip, B. G. (2002). Measuring culturally sensitive factors of classroom learning environments with the CLEQ. In Goh, S. C., & Myint, S. K. (Eds.) *Studies in Educational Learning Environments: An International Perspective* (pp. 27–48). Singapore: World Scientific Publishing.

Fisher, D. L., Fraser, B. J., & Rickards, T. (1997). Gender and Cultural Difference in Teacher-student Interpersonal Behaviour. Paper Presented at the Annual Meeting of the American Educational Research Associations, Chicago, IL.

Fraser, B. J. (1984). Differences between preferred and actual classroom environment as perceived by primary students and teachers. *British Journal of Educational Psychology*, 54, 336–339.

Fraser, B .J. (2002). Learning environments research: Yesterday, today and tomorrow. In Goh, S. C., & Myint, S. K. (Eds.) *Studies in Educational Learning Environments: An International Perspective* (pp. 1–26). Singapore: World Scientific.

Fraser, B. J., Giddings, G. J., & McRobbie, C. J. (1995). Evolution and validation of a personal form of an instrument for assessing science laboratory classroom environments. *Journal Research in Science Teaching*, 32, 399–422.

Fraser, B. J., Williamson, J.C., & Tobin, K. (1987). Use of classroom and school climate scales in evaluating alternative high schools. *Teaching and Teacher Education*, 3, 219–231.

Getzel, J. W., & Thelen, H. A. (1972). A conceptual framework for the study of the classroom group as a social system. In A. Morrison and D. McIntyre (Eds.), *The Social Psychology of Teaching* (pp. 17–34). Harmondsworth: Penguin.

Goh, C. T. (1997). Shaping our future: Thinking schools and a learning nation. *Speeches*, 21(3), 12–20.

Goh, S. C. (2002). Studies on learning environments in Singapore classrooms. In Goh, S.C., & Myint, S.K. (Eds.), *Studies in Educational Learning Environments: An International Perspective* (pp. 197–218). Singapore: World Scientific Publishing.

Goh, S. C., & Fraser, B. J. (2000). Teacher interpersonal behavior and elementary students' outcomes. *Journal of Research in Childhood Education*, 14(2), 216–231.

Henderson, D., Fisher, D., & Fraser, B. J. (1995). Gender differences in biology students' perceptions of actual and preferred learning environments. Paper Presented at the Annual Meeting of the National Association for Research in Science Teaching, San Francisco, CA.

Lee, S. L. (1997). Developing a shared nationhood. *Speeches*, 21(3), 41–52.

MOE (1998). *Desired Outcomes of Education.* Singapore: Ministry of Education.

MOE (1999). *Ability-driven Education.* Singapore: Ministry of Education.

Owen, L. C., & Straton, R. G. (1980). The development of cooperative, competitive and individualized learning preferences scale for students. *British Journal of Educational Psychology*, 50, 147–161.

Raviv, A., Raviv, A., & Reisel, E. (1990). Teacher and students: Two different perspectives measuring social climate in the classroom. *American Educational Research Journal*, 27, 387–393.

SEM (2003). *School Excellence Model.* Singapore: Ministry of Education.

Shechtman, Z. (2002). Child group psychotherapy in the school at the threshold of a new millenium. *Journal of Counseling & Development*, Summer, 80, 293–299.

Tan, A. G. (1999). An exploratory study of Singaporean student teachers' perception of teacher roles that are important in fostering creativity.'*Education Journal*, 27(2), 103–123.

Teo, C. H. (1997). Opening the frontiers in education with information technology. *Speeches*, 21(2), 92–98.

Walberg, H. J., & Anderson, G. J. (1968). Classroom climate and individual learning. *Journal of Educational Psychology*, 59, 414–419.

Welch, W. W., & Walberg, H.J. (1972). A national experiment in curriculum evaluation. *American Educational Research Journal*, 9, 373–383.

Wills, C. M. (1995). Creative Dance Education - Establishing a Positive Learning Environment, *JOPERD*, August, 16–20.

Wong, A. F. L., Young, D. J., & Fraser, B. J. (1997). A multilevel analysis of learning environment and student attitudes. *Educational Psychology*, 17(4), 449–468.

Woods, J., & Fraser, B. J. (1995). Utilizing Feedback Data on students' Perceptions of Teaching Style and Preferred Learning Style to Enhance Teaching Effectiveness. Paper Presented at the Annual meeting of the National Association for Research in Science teaching, San Francisco, CA.

Yee, F. W. C. (2003). *Student Perceptions of Choral Learning Environment* (Unpublished Master Dissertation). Singapore: National Institute of Education.

CHAPTER FIVE

Athey, C. (1990). *Extending Thought in Young Children.* London: Paul Chapman Publishing.

Bhabha, H. K. (1994). *The Location of Culture.* New York: Routledge.

Bouffard, T. (1998). A developmental study of the relationship between reading development and self-system. *European Journal of Educational Psychology*, 13(1), 61–74.

Bouffard, T., & Vezeau, C. (1998). The Developing self-system and self-regulation of primary school children. In M. D. Ferrari & R. J. Sternberg

(Eds.) *Self-Awareness: Its Nature and Development* (pp. 246–272). New York: The Guilford Press.

Cole, D. A., Maxwell, S. E., & Martin, J. M. (1997) Reflected self-appraisals: Strength and structure of the relation of teacher, peer, and parent ratings to children's self-perceived competence. *Journal of Educational Psychology*, 89(1), 55–70.

Dewey, J. (1884). The new psychology. *Andover Review*, 2, 278–289.

Diakidoy, I. A. N., & Kanari, E. (1999). Student teachers' beliefs about creativity. *British Educational Research Journal*, 25(2), 225–241.

Gupta, J. N. D., Sharma, S. K., & Hsu, J. (2004). An overview of knowledge management. In J. N. D. Gupta & S. K. Sharma (Eds.), *Creating Knowledge Based Organizations* (pp. 1–28). Hershey: Idea Group Publishing.

Gutierrez, K. D., Baqueodano-Lopez, P., Tejeda, C., & Rivera, A. (1999, April). Hybridity as a tool for understanding literacy learning. Paper presented at the American Educational Research Association, Montreal, Quebec, Canada.

Majo, E. B., Ciechanowski, K. M., Kramer, K., Ellis, L., Carrillo, R., & Collazo, T. (2004). Working toward third space in content area literacy: An examination of everyday funds of knowledge and discourse. *Reading Research Quarterly*, Jan-Mar, 39(1), 38–70.

Nelson, C. A., Monk, C. S., Lin, J., Carver, L. J., Thomas, K. M., & Truwit, C. L. (2000). Functional neuroanatomy of spatial working memory in children. *Developmental Psychology*, 36(1), 109–116.

Nieto, S. (1994). Lessons from students on creating a chance to dream. *Harvard Educational Review*, 64(4), 392–426.

Simonton, D. K. (1975). Sociocultural content of individual creativity: A transhistorical time-series analysis. *Journal of Personality and Social Psychology*, 32(6), 1119–1133.

Stipek, D., & MacIver, D. (1989) Developmental change in children's assessment of intellectual intelligence. *Child Development*, 60, 521–538.

Tan, A.G. (1998). Fostering students' creativity using learner-centered strategies. *SRL Magazine*, 10(4), 8–9.

Tan, A.G. (2003). Thinking Outside the Box: An Interview by Siew Mei Fong. *Motherhood Magazine*, May, 55–57.

Tan, A. G. (2004). Creativity in the classroom: An interview by Nisha Kalwani entitled ERAS 2003. *Voices*, 5, 7.

The New London Group (1996). A pedagogy of multiliteracies: Designing social futures. *Harvard Educational Review*, 66(1), 60–92.

EPILOGUE

Boyer, W. H. (2002). *Education for the Twenty-first Century*. San Fransisco, CA: Caddo Gap Press.

Deci, E. L., & Ryan, R. (1985). *Intrinsic Motivation and Self-Determination in Human Behavior*. New York: Plenum.

Goeker, J. (2003). Teaching for the future: Systems thinking and sustainability. *Green Teacher*, 70, 8–14.

Lamb, W. W. H. (2001). The "whole child" in education. *Journal of Philosophy of Education*, 35(2), 203–217.

Masschelein, J. (2001). The discourse of the learning society and the loss of childhood. *Journal of Philosophy of Education*, 35(1), 1–20.

Schantz, D., & Rideout, G. (2003). Education versus Schooling: Seeking new paradigms for a new century. *Education*, 124(1), 203–211.

Scott, W., & Gough, S. (2003). *Sustainable Development and Learning: Framing the Issues*. London: Routledge Falmer.

Seng, S. H. (2003). Promoting IT in childhood education: How Singapore prepares for the future. *Childhood Education*, 79(5), 283–286.

Sigworth, D., Hawkins, C., & Daiek, D. (2003). 21st century skills: Are we teaching what students need to know? *The Community College Enterprise*, 9(1), 39–47.

Tan, A.G. (1998). Fostering students' creativity using learner-centered strategies. *SRL Magazine*, 10(4), 8–9.

Index